W9-BBN-215

Advance praise for In the Company of the Poor

"Rarely have two such distinctive and complementary voices been raised together with more heartwarming and instructive results than here in *In the Company of the Poor*. Paul Farmer and Gustavo Gutiérrez share a deep commitment to 'pragmatic solidarity' with the poor and marginalized, whether in Lima's slums, or the rural reaches of Haiti or Rwanda, or in prisons or squatter settlements. This book is erudite, fresh, and even, at turns, witty; it draws in a lovely way on a deep friendship between physician and theologian. Their own friends will, I know, celebrate this book, which will introduce a broad audience to important notions, from accompaniment to a preferential option for the poor, which are transformed in this book into vivid examples not just of what's wrong with the world, but also what can be done to repair it."
—**Archbishop Desmond Tutu, Nobel Peace Laureate**

"It is a most rewarding experience to listen to two unusual and extraordinarily impressive people as their meditations and discussions guide us through the intricacies of accompanying the poor with 'meaningful dignified service to the oppressed' by a gifted physician who is truly engaged with their lives and future and examination of 'our own responsibility for the existence of *unjust social mechanisms*' by a founder of the remarkable movement of liberation theology."
—**Noam Chomsky, Professor Emeritus, MIT**

"These very warm, personal, and intimate testimonies take us into the loving heart of two very committed, beautiful and joyful friends of the poor and friends of God."
—**Virgilio Elizondo, Professor of Pastoral and Hispanic Theology, University of Notre Dame**

"An utterly captivating book. There is something in the warm conversational tone that opens a window to understanding ideas that heavier writing tends to obscure. Besides illuminating liberation theology's core concept of option for the poor, this lovely text also traces the influence of Gutiérrez as a mentor whose thinking inspires the good work of the younger Farmer. Their relationship as evidenced here is a treasure, and a source of hope."
—**Elizabeth Johnson, Distinguished Professor of Theology, Fordham University**

"This book beautifully proves what I have always thought, that Paul Farmer is prophetic. In his prior global health works, he repeatedly offered uncanny insights into the human condition. But this book is far more revelatory: it opens with his autobiographical witness to Gustavo Gutierrez's theology of liberation. Then there are the engagements, Paul of the theology, Gustavo of global health, but eventually they meet, in a way, the mentee and the mentor, two people, very different in age, background, and competency, conversing about what they each have learned from the poor about suffering, health, and hope: an historic, prophetic encounter."
—**James F. Keenan, S.J., Founders Professor in Theology, Boston College**

"These conversations between Gustavo Gutiérrez and Paul Farmer offer a compelling guide for analysis and action, transforming many preconceptions about how injustices are created, maintained and can be eliminated. Underlying the searing condemnations of unnecessary suffering and the explorations of a challenging path ahead, Gutiérrez and Farmer display deep and tender appreciation of humanity that every reader will find heart-opening. This sublime book is the one I would take to a desert island."
—Leslie Fleming, Director of Anthropology Program, Merritt College, Oakland, California

"*In the Company of the Poor* is so much more than a conversation between two great thinkers of our time. Brilliantly moving between Gutiérrez's arguments for the sacred and Farmer's for the secular, their conversation appeals to us to observe, judge, and act. The strength of *In the Company of the Poor* is its call for proximate action in all spheres, for diligent and discerning accompaniment of the locally poor, and advocacy directed at the globally powerful. Whether we want to call it mercy or solidarity, Farmer and Gutiérrez argue that to be for the poor is to not accept their poverty. Rather, action to remediate the structural violence at the root of poverty is an imperative. In the increasingly technocratic world we live in, this book is a balm."
—Salmaan Keshavjee MD, PhD, ScM, Director, Program in Infectious Disease and Social Change, Department of Global Health and Social Medicine, Harvard Medical School

"In this transformative book, Paul Farmer takes us with him to the poorest people on earth, victims of what he calls 'structural sin.' In his conversations with Father Gustavo Gutiérrez, Farmer invites us to respond with a fierce curiosity about the causes of poverty, and a new closeness to the poor, such as Farmer himself keeps, stethoscope on a tubercular child's chest. Then 'convert.' Convert? Yes. By applying the love we feel toward our own family, friends, and community to those who live with grime, despair and labored breathing. This is a must-read book by one—and about two—of the great human beings of our time."
—Arlie Hochschild, author, The Outsourced Self and So How's the Family? And Other Essays.

"Motivating reading for anyone concerned with public health in a world without borders and who struggles to understand and resolve the complex problems that emerge when our health systems are insufficiently creative or not flexible enough to address the demands of those living in poverty. Converts and those who are in the process of conversion will find, in reading this text, that there is still a long road to travel, but that their efforts surely will not be in vain. Thank you, Paul and Padre Gustavo, for sharing this book with us. It motivates and inspires."
—Jaime Bayona, Public Health Advisor, World Bank

In the Company of the Poor

In the Company of the Poor

Conversations between
Dr. Paul Farmer and Father Gustavo Gutiérrez

Edited by
Michael Griffin and Jennie Weiss Block

ORBIS BOOKS
Maryknoll, New York 10545

ORBIS BOOKS
Maryknoll, New York 10545

Fathers and Brothers
MARYKNOLL

Founded in 1970, Orbis Books endeavors to publish works that enlighten the mind, nourish the spirit, and challenge the conscience. The publishing arm of the Maryknoll Fathers and Brothers, Orbis seeks to explore the global dimensions of the Christian faith and mission, to invite dialogue with diverse cultures and religious traditions, and to serve the cause of reconciliation and peace. The books published reflect the views of their authors and do not represent the official position of the Maryknoll Society. To learn more about Maryknoll and Orbis Books, please visit our website atwww.maryknollsociety.org

Copyright © 2013 by Orbis Books

Published by Orbis Books, Box 302, Maryknoll, NY 10545-0302.

All rights reserved.

Gustavo Gutiérrez, "Conversion: A Requirement of Solidarity," is reprinted from *We Drink From Our Own Wells,* © 1984, 2003 by Orbis Books.

Paul Farmer, "Health, Healing, and Social Justice: Insights from Liberation Theology," is reprinted from *Pathologies of Power: Health, Human Rights, and the New War on the Poor* © 2003 with permission of the University of California Press.

Gustavo Gutiérrez, "The Option for the Poor Arises from Faith in Christ," is reprinted with permission of *Theological Studies.*

No part of this publication may be reproduced or transmitted in any form or by any means, electronic or mechanical, including photocopying, recording, or any information storage or retrieval system, without prior permission in writing from the publisher.

Queries regarding rights and permissions should be addressed to: Orbis Books, P.O. Box 302, Maryknoll, NY 10545-0302.

Manufactured in the United States of America

Library of Congress Cataloging-in-Publication Data

In the company of the poor : conversations between Dr. Paul Farmer and Fr. Gustavo Gutierrez / edited by Michael Griffin and Jennie Weiss Block.
      pages cm
   Includes index.
   ISBN 978-1-62698-050-1 (pbk.)
      1. Liberation theology.   2. Poverty—Religious aspects—Christianity.
3. Church work with the poor.   4. Farmer, Paul, 1959–   5. Gutiérrez, Gustavo,
1928–   I. Griffin, Michael.   II. Block, Jennie Weiss.
BT83.57.I5 2013
261.8'325—dc23

2013014506

Contents

Foreword

Father Bruno Cadoré, OP
Master of the Order of Preachers

We must fight poverty, and the time is now! Throughout this conversation between Dr. Paul Farmer and Father Gustavo Gutiérrez, this conviction is made manifest. Naturally, the two authors arrive at this point by way of different commitments. Gutiérrez developed his proposals for a liberation theology in the course of a human, pastoral struggle with the structural poverty affecting so many people in the cities of South America. Farmer was faced with the scandal of inequality in health care, in countries where most people do not even have access to primary care, and he was led to act in the domains of treatment and public health. Both of them, experiencing the "insomnia of the scandal of poverty," express a similar understanding of the logic of the contemporary world(s), and their experience leads them to call on human creativity for "critical practices" that can accomplish a reversal of the very world logics that produce and shore up unjust structures of poverty. Their dialogue recalls their individual experiences, both of them marked by the encounter with a great store of human generosity seeking to change the world in concrete and organized ways, and marked as well by the travails of solidarity born of the irrevocable call to honor the dignity of every human being as well as the dignity of different human societies.

As it often happens, the harmony between two friends is to some degree given, sealed, by an urgent concern for mutual friends. These are, first, the poor, the sick, those left on the margins of the "mainstream" of our globalized world, the victims of the structures responsible for poverty and marginalization, logics that, with the indifferent arrogance of power, released from criticism and unjust, do violence to the most vulnerable, making them victims of injustice and, by this very victimization, more and more vulnerable. But the world itself is another mutual friend of these two friends, a world for which they share the hope that this world may, relying on the human capacity for goodness and intelligence, transform itself into a genuinely "hospitable world for the human species."

This conversation between friends is thus an invitation extended to the contemporary worlds themselves, an invitation to open dialogue among them. A friendly dialogue is always marked with the seal of hospitality, with the invitation extended to each and every one to enter into the human conversation in which, by the exchange of words, humans teach one another that the first responsibility of a human being is to offer humanness to one's fellows. The authors of this book attest that this mutual hospitality cannot occur without giving primacy to those who, most often, are forgotten and relegated to the "far side of the world."

It is from this "far side of the world"—which might turn out to be its nearest "near side"—that the authors call on the world to have a conversation with itself. How can I fail to evoke the words with which, fifty years ago, Pope Paul VI called on the church to remake herself as dialogue and conversation? What could constitute this "conversation of the world"? In a prefatory way, and without any claim to offer an exhaustive synthesis of the texts that follow, I would like to mention some characteristic features of the dialogue proposed in this book.

First comes the determination to call the world not to desert itself, and for this, not to let indifference possess those who are victims of political, social, and economic logics of which they are neither the deciders nor the beneficiaries. The reality of the poor neighborhoods where so many Christians have experienced the presence of the promise made by the biblical God not to abandon those God loves, has been the crucible in which liberation theology has sought to interpret this promise. Confrontation with the terrible realities of sickness and death caused by inability to access primary care and prevention measures has only reinforced the conviction that medicine requires us to care for people and simultaneously to take care of the quality of hospitality in our societies. With Paul Ricoeur, one could say that the experience of friendship with the poor, of trust shared with them, is as it were an imperative to humanity not to forsake what constitutes it: its capacity of concern for the other and the demand to extend this concern to social structures.

The common point of these two experiences is that this "nonindifference to the other" hinges on the dynamic of an "economy of dignity." To be sure, fighting poverty means giving honor and reverence to the irreducible and inalienable dignity of every human being, on the same footing as any other, without regard to individuals, conditions, race, gender, talents, power, or wealth. But the imperative to demand this unconditional respect for the dignity of every person does not derive from a logical deduction: it is based on encountering the scandalous reality of "disrespected" dignity that provokes in the human being the conviction that this "disrespect" "disrespects" humanity as a whole. The economy of dignity is the movement by which nonindifference leads us to choose, once and for all, the side of shared destinies, in the name of a common humanity. When someone is the victim of a scandalous degree of poverty that he can do nothing about, when a child falls victim to tuberculosis because nothing has been planned against it, when someone dies of hunger or malaria because social structures are not concerned by these realities—such cases of "collateral damage" spawned by the arrogant logic of the production of wealth and security for a few harm not only this or that human being but human

dignity as a whole. What is at stake is the dignity of human
sociality itself.

A third characteristic feature of the dialogue between medicine
and liberation theology is the urgency of developing critical practices of struggle against poverty. Such social or medical practices
have as their first aim to restore, as far as possible, the balance in
favor of those who in this world are victims of poverty, marginalized, humiliated, destroyed, put in danger, excluded. From
this point of view, the oft-invoked notion of priority becomes
understandable: it is not a matter of declaring a hierarchy of
worth, but a hierarchy of emergencies. The effort to restore balance,
including measures of preference given to those who are the
most marginalized, is a first step toward justice. But the press-

ing need is not only to act "for" them, in order to reestablish
conditions for the full unfolding of their capacities to be actors
of their own history. It is also and especially to act "with" them,
for solidarity in practices of world transformation is what can
truly testify to the conviction of a common dignity, a solidarity
in the advancement of the necessary conditions for the unfolding
of the full dignity of human sociality.

As I read the pages of these two authors, I had the feeling
that we were located "somewhere in the incomplete," to use the
expression of the philosopher Vladimir Jankélévitch. We are located in a place of humanity where the incompleteness of human
sociality is revealed not as lack but as plenty, a call to inspire sociality with the desire to advance always further in the dynamism
of this economics of dignity. The human race cannot know its
own future. Humanity can probably not even claim to define for
itself and build on its own whatever it is called to become. But
the imperative of solidarity, of this solidarity that in some way
restores all humanity in its capacity of mutual hospitality, draws
us into these practices by which, starting with a struggle against
poverty side by side with poor people, the human being can begin
to hope to see the full realization of this sociality. Through this
aspiration, through this desire, the practices of solidarity make

clear to human beings that they are, as it were, stepping in the prior traces of a sociality not made by human hands, but one that makes possible, or more accurately makes imperative, the engagement of nonindifference to the fate of the dignity of historical human sociality. The practices of solidarity, practices that are simultaneously a critical hermeneutics of the dominant logics of the world, inscribe in the heart of humanity the desire of a sociality that humanity would not be capable of building, of mastering, or even of totally annihilating. In the field of theology, could this longed-for sociality not be called communion, the archetype of the Covenant promised by the God of biblical revelation, and accomplished by the Son when his friendship with the poor led him to choose sides against the powers of falsehood, to cause the light of truth to break out of his kenosis?

From this point of view, the practices of solidarity with the poor, in the struggle against the structures of poverty designed to keep them "outside the global mainstream," could well be mediations of the mystery of a truth that makes free.

Acknowledgments

It has been a privilege and a joy to be a part of this conversation between Dr. Paul Farmer and Fr. Gustavo Gutiérrez. It has also been a wonderful opportunity for their respective teams, friends and institutions to collaborate on a common project; one that we hope and believe will bear much fruit. Many people have accompanied us throughout the process of the writing, editing, and production of this book, and while this list could surely be much longer, a few special thanks are in order.

To the Notre Dame University community and especially the Kellogg Institute for International Studies, for their gracious welcome and for providing the perfect environment for the conversations that are the foundation of this book.

To all those who helped to make the 2011 Fall Conference an unqualified success especially Dan Groody, CSJ, and Tony Pohlen, and for those who traveled to be with us during those special days including Lisbee Munford, Nancy Dorsinville, and Jon Weigel.

To the members of Fr. Gustavo's "Christian Spirituality and the Transformation of History" course, and to students Mary Atwood and Joseph Vander Zee, for providing the choir at Mass in the Log Chapel at Notre Dame.

To Bill Groody of Groody River Productions for providing the audio production for the interview between Dr. Farmer and Fr. Gustavo, and to Janet McCormick and Rosabelle Conover for transcription assistance.

To Paul's great team in Boston at Partners In Health, Harvard Medical School, and the Brigham and Woman's Hospital especially Mary Block, Jon Niconchuk and Kevin Savage for their work on this project.

To all of Paul's colleagues who have worked untiringly to translate the theological concept of a preferential option for the poor into daily global health praxis especially Paul's earliest supporter, Tom White whose presence continues to inspire us in death as it did in life, Ophelia Dahl, Jim Kim, Todd McCormack, Didi Bertrand, the community at St. Mary of the Angels, Mercedes Becerra, Jaime Bayona, Shamsher Samra, Barbara Rylko-Bauer, Nancy Scheper-Hughes, Jim Keenan, SJ, Mike Westerhaus, and to Paul's many students through the years who appreciate and engage the link between liberation theology and social medicine.

To our friends at Barry University in Miami, especially Jim Nicoloff, Mark Wedig, OP and Jorge Presmanes, OP, for their on-going support of our work and for providing yet another location to continue the Gutiérrez/Farmer conversation.

To Matt Ashley and John Cavadini of Notre Dame Theology Department for their welcome and on-going support of Fr. Gustavo, and to all who have provided hospitality to Paul especially Ann and Todd McCormack, Bill Helman, Laurie Nuell, and Jeff Farmer.

To Steve Reifenberg, Christine Cervenak and their family for their support of this project and for their on-going commitment to the well-being of the world's poorest people.

To Robert Ellsberg and Orbis Books for their interest in and support of the conversation between Paul Farmer and Gustavo Gutiérrez; we are thrilled to be working with you.

Two individuals deserve particular acknowledgement. First, to Professor Haun Saussy, Paul's life-long editor and devoted friend. Haun's editorial skill and speed are unmatched, and his generosity and kindness legendary. We are grateful for his presence in our lives and for his fine translation of Fr. Bruno Caldoré's preface, and the wonderful editing of the Gutiérrez/Farmer interview—one of the highlights of this book. And second, to Catherine

Griffin for her support, patience and good humor. Throughout the many months that her husband Michael was busy laboring as editor on this book project, she labored right alongside of him with her own community project. It was with great joy that we welcomed and celebrated the birth of Basil James Griffin on January 20,, 2013. Congratulations to Mike, Catherine and big brother, Benedict. Fr. Gustavo will soon be baptizing baby Basil just as he baptized Benedict two years ago, and we look forward to watching their two sons grow in wisdom and grace.

And, finally, all associated with this book, especially its editors, thank Paul Farmer and Gustavo Gutiérrez for letting all of us share in the joy of writing this very special book. We are grateful to have been in your company.

Jennie Weiss Block, OP
Coral Gables, Florida

Michael Griffin
South Bend, Indiana

July 2013

Introduction

Jennie Weiss Block and Michael Griffin

> There is a criterion for knowing whether God is close to us or far away: all those who worry about the hungry, the naked, the poor, the disappeared, the tortured, the imprisoned—about any suffering human being—are close to God.
>
> —*Archbishop Oscar Romero*

Of Two Worlds and One Mind

Paul Farmer was born in North Adams, Massachusetts, in 1959, the same year that Gustavo Gutiérrez turned thirty-one and was ordained a priest. Gustavo grew up in Lima, Peru, in a close-knit family in humble circumstances. A promising student, Gustavo was the first in his family to go to college with plans to become a doctor but instead entered the seminary in response to his call to the priesthood. Paul grew up in Central Florida on the edge of a swamp, living in a bus with his parents and five siblings. As Paul's unusual but nonetheless stable childhood unfolded, the newly ordained Father Gustavo was busy pastoring a large parish in the slums on the outskirts of Lima, Peru. Separated by generation, culture, and country, the two worlds that formed Paul Farmer and Gustavo Gutiérrez couldn't have been more different: truly parallel universes. This book, however, is not about their

Jennie Weiss Block, OP, serves as Chief Advisor to Dr. Paul Farmer.
Michael Griffin teaches theology at Holy Cross College in Notre Dame, Indiana.

differences but rather about what these two extraordinary men have in common, namely, an uncommon dedication to accompanying the poor of this world on the path from oppression to liberation.

Paul was eleven years old in 1971 when Father Gustavo's seminal text *A Theology of Liberation: History, Politics and Salvation* was published. The new and daring ideas put forth in a theology of liberation, with its interpretation of the Christian faith from the perspective of the suffering poor, forged a new theological discourse that would give voice to millions of people who were previously, as Father Gustavo puts it, "absent from the pages of history." Resonating far beyond its birthplace in Latin America, liberation theology would be adopted by others whose life experiences have been marked by oppression, poverty, and exclusion, such as North American feminists and Latina *mujeristas*, gays and lesbians, blacks, and people with disabilities—to mention a few. The advent of liberation theology also permanently altered the perspectives and practices of those attempting to live the Christian life in a serious way. Although concern and care for the poor have always constituted a central tenet of what it means to be Christian, the pointed question of *why* billions of people live in abject and dire poverty had not yet been asked in a comprehensive fashion. The insights resulting from this line of questioning led believers away from a singular focus on personal sin and individual atonement toward what Donald Gelpi, SJ, called a "socio-political conversion." This conversion, taken up in its fullest sense by liberation theology, would insist that the Christian faithful acknowledge there are terribly sinful consequences deeply embedded in the way our prevailing social systems operate, and that the Christian life mandates solidarity with the poor through social and political action.

A dedicated guidance counselor at Paul's high school in Brooksville, Florida, saw in him great potential, and she and other teachers helped him earn a scholarship to Duke University. When Paul reached Duke in 1978, liberation theology was already gaining momentum and Father Gustavo was becoming well known in theological and church circles. At Duke, Paul voraciously read anthropology, history, sociology, and the basic sciences and sought explanations, inspiration, and mentorship as he tried to chart a course for his life and develop plans for his future.

Two formative events significantly influenced Paul during his college years. The first event occurred when Archbishop Oscar Romero of El Salvador was gunned down while celebrating the Eucharist in March of 1980. Paul was twenty years old when he heard the dramatic narrative of Romero's witness to the faith and his willingness to risk his life to challenge the prevailing social circumstances that kept his people poor and oppressed. Deeply moved by Romero's witness to the faith, Paul realized the impact that living a radical Christian life could have on the plight of the poor, and this gave him a new interest and respect for the Catholic faith of his childhood and a home for his own spiritual yearnings and desire to serve.

Second, he started writing about migrant farm workers and about a "social justice nun" (as he affectionately called Sr. Julianna DeWolf) and her ministry among migrant farmworkers. He appreciated Sr. Julianna's militant tendencies and willingness to do any job—however menial—to help those she served. Sr. Julianna would be the first of many nuns and priests with whom Paul would partner in one way or another in the years to come. While observing Sr. Julianna, Paul had his first "contrast experience." Paul saw the hard life of the migrant workers, invisible on the margins of society, living just a few miles down the road from his own comfortable life on a campus where everyone had access to food, housing, education, medical care, and every kind of opportunity for personal fulfillment. He knew that something was fundamentally wrong. He saw the nuns siding with the poor and abused. Seeing social inequality and injustice firsthand motivated him to think about how he might work for change.

An ancient proverb asserts, "When the pupil is ready, the master appears." And, so it was when Father Gustavo's book, *A The-*

ology of Liberation found its way into Paul Farmer's hands in Haiti over a decade after it was first published. In Gutiérrez's generative treatise calling for a "preferential option for the poor," a young Paul Farmer found a worthy organizing principle for his life's work. Paul so internalized Father Gustavo's thinking that he chose a "preferential option for the poor in health care" as the mission statement for Partners In Health, the NGO he cofounded in Boston in 1987. Although Paul would not meet Father Gustavo in person until 1994, Father Gustavo became a significant mentor. As Paul began to publish scholarly papers and books, Gutiérrez quotes would grace his pages, and the "option for the poor" would animate his thinking and inform his work as a physician.

In 1994, Dr. Farmer and Father Gustavo would finally meet in Peru, forming a deep and abiding friendship that has continued to grow over the next three decades. Their differences in age, country, culture, and career paths seem minor in comparison to all they share. Marked by deep respect on both the personal and professional levels, their great friendship finds its expression in the shared goal of a life lived in pursuit of a preferential option for the poor. The ways in which their disciplines have intersected is mutually satisfying and validating. Dr. Farmer is indebted to Father Gustavo for his mentorship and for his moral clarity. The ways in which Dr. Farmer has used liberation theology to frame and guide his medical work is a source of great joy for Father Gustavo, and he will always be grateful to Paul and to Partners In Health for worldwide work in health care and social justice, especially in his own beloved Peru.

A Shared Moral Imagination

The term "moral imagination" was coined by Edmund Burke (1727–1797) to describe the way in which wisdom and virtue can be joined together to create a vision of the way in which a humane life is to be lived. Exercising one's "moral imagination" necessarily involves, in the words of David Tracy, "risking a norm," that is, being willing to make normative claims about what is good, right, and just. Father Gustavo and Dr. Farmer do not shrink from making such claims in both theory and praxis: the clear cry for "a preferential option for the poor" does not tilt toward moral relativism. Their voices, actions, intellectual discipline, and commitment of time and treasure flesh out a moral life that many find worth emulating. In particular, the Gutiérrez/Farmer moral imagination shares four concrete expressions: first, a lifelong commitment to accompany the poor in their daily struggles; second, raising a prophetic voice in the public square—no matter what the cost; third, integrating theory and praxis; and fourth, building up the Kingdom of God in the here and now.

Accompanying the Poor

Both Father Gustavo and Dr. Farmer have lived among the poor for all of their adult lives. Both have shared life with the poor at its deepest and most intimate levels—as priest, as doctor, as friend, as confidant. Father Gustavo explains it well when he says, "If there is no friendship with the poor and no sharing of the life of the poor, then there is no authentic commitment to liberation, because love exists only among equals."[1] Both acknowledge the poor as their greatest teachers and a constant source of inspiration. Father Gustavo is first a pastoral minister in his parish church in the slums of Lima, and only second a world-renowned scholar, professor, and author. Never have his academic tasks taken him for long away from his people. Even now, in his mid-eighties, Father Gustavo spends half of each year away from Notre Dame and working in his parish in the slums of Lima. Dr. Farmer moved into a little house in a squatter settlement in the Central Plateau of Haiti in his mid-twenties where he worked side by side with the Haitian poor to build a community infrastructure that would include a hospital and a school. Legend has it that he spent more time in Haiti than he did in Boston when he was attending Harvard Medical School. Although his work as a physician takes him to many countries around the globe, where for long and short periods of time he lives and works among the poor, he still calls his little house in Cange, Haiti, home.

Both Father Gustavo and Dr. Farmer thus subscribe to what they call a "theology of accompaniment." The practice of accompaniment is highly personal and deeply relational. Accompaniment of the lonely poor involves walking with—not behind or in front—but beside a real person on his or her own particular journey in his or her own particular place and time, at his or her own particular pace. Accompanying others in their struggles for survival does not have a beginning or an end, and there is no outside plan to be imposed. It often means being present to terrible suffering, being thrown into chaotic circumstances, encountering unexpected problems and difficult situations with no easy solutions. And yet, accompaniment, the act of "walking with another" is, in the words of Roberto Goizueta, "always a fundamentally religious sacramental act."[2] The lived experience of Father Gustavo and Dr. Farmer bear witness to the grace and mystery of this accompanying presence.

Raising a Prophetic Voice in the Public Square

Across a wide span of decades and continents and contexts, Father Gustavo and Dr. Farmer have boldly proclaimed the scandalous reality that "things are not as they should be. Billions of people live in crushing poverty without access to the goods and services that make human flourishing possible. What are we doing wrong? How can things be righted?" They have brought this message to bear in every "public square" they can garner—in their extensive bodies of writing, in the classrooms of the best universities in the world, in the corridors of power where the powerful gather to create laws and policies, in squatter settlements, in hospitals and clinics where both the rich and poor seek medical treatment, at fund-raising dinners with wealthy donors, in interviews with the media, at ceremonies where they accept prestigious awards and honors, always on behalf of the poor—essentially anywhere two or three are gathered and willing to listen.

Those who systematically challenge the dominant political and cultural structures tend to cause a stir. Raising topics that call for the redistribution of power and upset the status quo comes at a certain price. Giving voice to the voiceless and making the privileged class uncomfortable is risky business, and both Father Gustavo and Dr. Farmer have not been without critics for championing these causes. Though never rejected by church authorities, and even incorporated into Catholic social doctrine, the liberation theology of Gutiérrez is a lightning rod for those uninterested in a Christian critique of capitalism or in the exploration of the political dimensions of following Jesus. And although Dr. Farmer's work in bringing health care to the poorest people in the world has been heralded as a noble enterprise, questions inevitably rise, after the compliments, about cost-effectiveness and sustainability (code for the lives of the poor are not worth as much as the lives of the rich). Both men understand well the political implications of their actions but have rarely let fear of negative consequences deter their prophetic stance.

Integrating Theory and Praxis

Liberation theology begins with the task of critically reflecting on praxis in the light of faith. Done by scholars and academicians, this important work, first, exposes difficult or inconvenient truths such as how current policies, practices, and structures are contributing to the oppression of millions of people, and second, offers critical reflections that lead to new theoretical insights and ultimately direct renewed praxis. Unfortunately, there is, all too often, a disconnect between theory and its practical applications in the field. In other words, there is not a clear link between scholarship and implementation. Realizing how critical the integration of theory and praxis is, Dr. Farmer and Father Gustavo have forged an unusual career path as both scholars and implementers.

Both Father Gustavo and Dr. Farmer have made pioneering academic contributions to their respective disciplines. Father Gustavo will always be known as the "father of liberation theology" and credited with giving us a new way to do theology that recognizes a God who takes the side of the poor and vulnerable. Dr. Farmer will always be credited for bringing the nineteenth-century notion of "social medicine" (and medical anthropology) into the mainstream of public health and creating an entire academic discipline dedicated to making access to medical care a human right. Both men are highly respected scholars and teachers holding chairs: Father Gustavo at Notre Dame and Dr. Farmer at Harvard. Each has authored numerous books and hundreds of articles, and both have garnered an impressive list of academic credentials and accomplishments. Although most academicians are content to leave the hard work of implementation to experienced practitioners in the field, what sets Dr. Farmer and Father Gustavo apart from other scholars is the way in which they are actively engaged in *both* the academic task and the implementation phase—in other words, they both reflect on suffering and respond to suffering. Understanding that liberation theologies always favor the primacy of praxis, the world beyond the academy is of paramount importance to them because that is where practical transformation occurs and where the lives of real people are improved. Even on a good day, balancing the rigors of academic life and the grinding work of implementation in the developing world is not an easy task, which makes their documented successes in the field all the more extraordinary.

Building up the Kingdom of God in the Here and Now

Father Gustavo often remarks that Jesus began his public ministry with these words: "Now is the time of fulfillment. The Kingdom of God is at hand" (Mk 1:15). Dr. Farmer and Father Gustavo take these words to heart and hear them as a personal call; so all they do, in a very real sense, is done to build up the Kingdom of God in the here and now—every day for real people in real places all over the globe. They soundly reject the notion that the poor will get their reward in heaven and should patiently accept their lot in this life. They know human suffering caused by human action (or inaction) is never acceptable and is contrary to the will of God. Paul Farmer points out that "even though it may seem like it to some, there is not a first world and a third world. There is only one world that we all share." Implied in this comment is the imperative that those with plenty had better make sure to share with those who go without.

Father Gustavo and Dr. Farmer are hope givers extraordinaire. One might think that constant exposure to grinding poverty, dealing with difficult situations with no easy solutions, long hours of hard work, and inevitable setbacks might make one depressed or negative. But it seems to be quite the opposite, for they share a cheerful countenance and radiate a certain joy that draws people to them—both those fortunate enough to know them personally and those who know them by reputation and through their writings. In a world desperate for meaning, it is easy to understand why people of all walks of life are drawn to Paul Farmer and Gustavo Gutiérrez, for they are filled with hope, and their sense of hope is contagious. However, they do not peddle a shallow optimism or a faux sense of cheerfulness or subscribe to, in the words of Dietrich Bonhoeffer, "cheap grace." No, the hope they offer is rugged and demanding and with a moral edge that cannot help but call us to conversion. It is a hope that has its origins in the Crucified One who emptied himself with a radical outpouring of love, and it is rooted in the firm belief that we are called to build the Kingdom of God in the here and now.

A Shared Conversation

This book is a conversation between two of the great men of our times. It is an in-depth conversation that begins from their particular perspectives—liberation theology and social medicine, respectively—but continues into the much wider territory of a consideration of the most pressing moral and ethical dilemmas that our world faces today: specifically, how to actively and effectively accompany people out of poverty and oppression.

This book is intended for a wide variety of audiences. It is intended for those who are committed to the hard work of building a just world, regardless of profession, training, or religious affiliation. We believe that theologians and medical professionals will find the intersections and practical applications of the work of two of their most distinguished colleagues interesting and inspiring. We hope that those working in nonprofit organizations or public institutions with oppressed and marginalized people in the United States and the developing world will be nourished by the creative and interdisciplinary work shared by a doctor and a theologian. This book can also be a resource for students of medicine, public health, anthropology, political science, philosophy, theology, community development, and economics, as they discern and prepare for their own life's work.

The book is organized in the following way. We begin with the words of these two men spoken in the presence of each other in front of a packed auditorium at Notre Dame. Farmer's tribute to Gutiérrez sets our context, highlighting why the work of the Peruvian theologian is clearly relevant to the challenge of the emerging field of public health. Gutiérrez's words then follow in Chapter 2, presenting his basic articulation of how concern for human suffering and injustice has been at the heart of Christian faith from the very beginning. In fact, this chapter brings to the fore a key concept of Gutiérrez's: that spirituality is not a theoretical matter, but rather involves the praxis of putting into action the faith we have in Jesus' proclamation of a new world.

Chapters 3 and 4 present classic texts from these two prolific authors. In "Health, Healing, and Social Justice: Insights from Liberation Theology," from his book *Pathologies of Power*, Farmer gives us a ground-level view of his work in social medicine and how it was transformed in concrete instances by insights gained from reading Gutiérrez's work. In particular, Farmer starkly challenges the model of "leftover medicine" that has dominated the efforts of those trying to bring charity into the health field. In "Conversion: A Requirement for Solidarity," from his classic book *We Drink from Our Own Wells*, Gutiérrez presents a radical challenge of his own. To those engaged in the struggle for human rights and social justice, he says our work will fail if it neglects the call to conversion in our own lives. We must cultivate a gratuitous love, which pushes even beyond the demands of justice, in order for justice to be properly appreciated and pursued.

We then present one of the new treasures of this book. In 2013, Farmer brought Father Gustavo's classic text with him on a work trip to Africa. He had read it as a young man and was returning to it roughly twenty years later for a new, reflective reading. His response, in the chapter titled "Conversion in the Time of Cholera," links the notion of conversion to broader concepts of social change. Farmer insists that the dismantling of social and political structures that perpetuate poverty requires conversion of both the people and the institutions that created them and those who study them too. His response illuminates the ways in which liberation theology has given moral framing to his life's work and how Father Gustavo's call for a "preferential option for the poor" became the central tenet of his and his colleagues' approach to global health care delivery.

In Chapter 6, we encounter Gustavo Gutiérrez in the quintessential practice of his craft. "The Option for the Poor Arises from

Faith in Christ" is a theologically rich defense of the principle for which Gutiérrez has become known: following Jesus involves, as a necessity, *the preferential option for the poor.* We explicitly chose not to begin with this text, even though its ideas are central. We knew that many nontheologians, especially those in the fields of medicine and public health, would be reading this book and might appreciate first having the context for Gutiérrez's paradigm-shifting work before delving headlong into a text originally written for other theologians but now applicable to readers of this book. In demonstrating that the church's profession of faith and promotion of justice are the same commitment, Gutiérrez emerges in this text as an impassioned theologian working to preserve the social soul of his tradition.

The closing chapter is, in many ways, the raison d'être and crowning achievement of this book. With the help of many others, both at Notre Dame and at Partners In Health, we have distilled into one text the highlights of the conversation between Farmer and Gutiérrez during their days together. Knowing the historic nature of their shared time, we were at the ready with recording devices of every sort as we tracked them from lunch tables to classrooms to interviews. Our main opportunity came when the two sat together and talked for three hours at Corby Hall, the priests' residence where Gutiérrez lives when he is at Notre Dame. From this rich material, we have selected the insights and exchanges that best capture the professional, intellectual, personal, and joyful relationship that has been forged by these two luminous figures who have become co-conspirators in the work of building a more just world.

Although much of his book thus comes from their days together at Notre Dame, in reality the conversation began long ago on that day when Paul Farmer opened, in rural Haiti, the pages of *A Theology of Liberation.* The dialogue has steadily continued for almost thirty years in the words of dozens of books and hundreds of articles, and in visits together all over the world. The two of us have no doubt the conversation will continue until Paul and Gustavo break bread together at the heavenly banquet in the fullness of the Kingdom of God.

A Shared Affection

The central event of their Notre Dame encounter was a joint public presentation, billed as "Re-imagining Accompaniment: Global Health and Liberation Theology." The huge auditorium in DeBartolo Hall was packed, and the event was live-streamed far and wide, including to a large group gathered at Harvard and Partners In Health. There was a buzz of excitement in the room as more people tried to find a seat on the floor or a place to stand in the back. Those lucky enough to be in South Bend had come to see and hear two of their heroes—live, onstage, together. They were seated on a raised platform, Father Gustavo in his navy blue sweater, and Dr. Farmer wearing his signature (and only) blue blazer and a tie embroidered with Dominican shields in honor of Father Gustavo's own membership in the Order of Preachers. Dr. Farmer often speaks on college campuses around the country and draws huge crowds of young people—flocking to a model for their own lives. However, on this particular evening, no one was more excited to be on the dais than Dr. Farmer—for he had come to be with and pay tribute to his own mentor and friend. Paul's love and admiration for Gustavo was evident to all present—both in the words of his tribute and in the sheer joy of his countenance.

The days together at Notre Dame were filled with teaching, visiting with friends and colleagues, shared meals, walks in the crisp fall weather on the beautiful campus, and of course, lots of time for conversation. It was abundantly clear to all that these two fine men relished their time together. The visit ended with a celebration of the Eucharist on Paul's fifty-second birthday in the historic Log Chapel at Notre Dame—the site where local Native Americans once came for spiritual care, medical resources, and accompaniment. In that chapel, with Father Gustavo's students as the choir and Dr. Farmer as the lector, all of us gathered knew that we were experiencing something special. Here were two of the most accomplished men of our age, sharing with others the simple and profound acts of the Eucharist: exchanging gestures of peace, listening to words of justice, drinking from the cup of salvation, and eating the bread of life. Indeed, sharing bread together—in Latin, *cum pane*—is the original meaning of the word accompaniment. It is our hope that this book, the culmination of bread shared by these two men and the people with whom they have lived and worked, will serve as nourishment for our own journeys and give us strength to join Paul Farmer and Gustavo Gutiérrez in building a just world—thy Kingdom come—where poverty and oppression are relics of the past.

Notes

[1] Gustavo Gutiérrez, *A Theology of Liberation* (Maryknoll, NY: Orbis Books, 1973), xxxi.

[2] Roberto S. Goizueta, *Caminemos con Jesus: Toward a Hispanic/Latino Theology of Accompaniment* (Maryknoll, NY: Orbis Books, 1995), 209.

1

Reimagining Accompaniment

A Doctor's Tribute to Gustavo Gutiérrez

Paul Farmer

In 1971, when Gustavo Gutiérrez published *A Theology of Liberation*, I was eleven years old and living in small-town Florida. To me, and to my siblings, church was a place one went to fulfill obligations to parents and grandparents: First Communion, Confirmation, high holy days. It meant sitting through homilies—often boring ones, I'm sorry to say, and almost always remote from our experience. Perhaps the priests made too little effort, or felt little need to make the effort, to address people our age; more likely, we made too little effort ourselves. The arcana of theology were of course completely beyond us. Once we had advanced to high school, we saw little reason to continue going to Mass. Our parents, who shared our ambivalence, did not insist.

A few years later, the boundaries of my world had expanded significantly. I was a college student in Durham, North Carolina, and learning at last about the world we inhabited, pushing back the boundaries so that more and more of this very real world was revealed to me. I learned about conflicts taking place in Central America. For me and most of my college peers, those conflicts were remote and hard to understand. But in fact they were so profoundly connected to our world that a journalist reporting the Salvadoran army's massacre of an entire village in that beleaguered nation would discover that the headstamps on the bullets read Lake City, Missouri.[1] I learned about the resistance to tyranny and

15

violence offered by many members of the church and thought: same church, same world. Not two or three worlds, but one. I stood in front of the Duke Chapel with more than a hundred fellow mourners, gathered in shock to grieve for the murder of Archbishop Oscar Romero of San Salvador. He had been cut down in the middle of Mass while intoning the very words, no doubt, that had recently seemed to me so dull and uninspiring.

After graduation, I spent the better part of a year in Haiti. If conflicts in distant countries were what it had taken to revive my interest in Catholic social teaching, proximity to suffering and poverty taught me even more about what these lessons might mean in the last years of the twentieth century. And it was the patient, scholarly work of Gustavo Gutiérrez that helped me make sense of the poverty I saw around me in Haiti, elsewhere in Latin America, and back home in the United States.

Understanding poverty as "structured evil," and understanding how it is perpetuated, is not the same as fighting it. But if we believe that knowledge can inform practice—if we believe in pragmatic solidarity as the best confirmation of theory—then it is best to have intellectual accompaniment. I have had Father Gustavo as my *accompagnateur* for many long years, including the decade before I had the chance to meet him in person.

Let me give an example. One day, early in my stay in rural Haiti, I was in my room in the rectory of an Episcopal Church in Mirebalais, a market town in the center of the country. I'd spent the day in a hot, overcrowded clinic. My job was to take vital signs, and to give moral support to the beleaguered young Haitian physician in charge. We quickly became good friends. In time he confessed how much he hated the work he had been called to do: "It's like a mediocre medical factory. No lab. No real chance to examine the patients or do more than the most perfunctory work." But he never did much to change it. These conditions were seemingly as immovable as fate. Not yet thirty, the doctor had been socialized for scarcity and failure, I came to understand, even as I had been socialized for plenty and success.

In other words, poverty had worked its way into the doctor's life too, even though he was not poor. This is exactly what is meant by the concept of structural violence: inequity that is "nobody's fault," that is just "the way things are," that we live with because we cannot or will not or do not know how to address the conditions that create unequal outcomes for rich and poor.[2] This idea, of an unjust social order that was in itself a form of structured violence, seeped into my consciousness throughout that year. It was, incidentally, one of the last years of the Duvalier family dictatorship.

Late on that Wednesday afternoon, after a copious meal (the two of us never lacked for food and clean water), we repaired to our rooms to read. I heard a ruckus outside. A crowd was chanting, marching down the street. The food riots and political demonstrations that would bring down the dictatorship were still more than a year away, and noises like this were almost always associated with some sort of local unpleasantness. I could hear the crowd very well.

Madame Providence manje de ti moun.

I knew enough Creole to know that the crowd was singing, "Mme Providence ate two children," and had read enough about Haiti to know that this was likely a sorcery accusation. I looked out and saw a crowd of people, pushing and pummeling a woman as they paraded her down the street toward the police station and could envision the fate reserved for her. I learned later that she was arrested on God-knows-what charges, and her beatings continued in the foul jail down the road. The brutality of it all revolted me. And what made me feel really lonely was that almost everyone I worked with, including the talented young doctor, seemed to take it all in stride, or to agree that Mme Providence might indeed have performed some sort of magical poisoning that felled a neighbor's two previously healthy children. "Who knows?" he asked, an eyebrow arched.

I did not, and still do not, believe in sorcery; I see accusations of sorcery as one outcome of injustices and local misfortunes that people endure until they can endure them no longer. By then I had seen kids die of malaria and of other acute infections. But how to explain all of this to myself or to others? The Haitian priest with whom I worked, and still work, dismissed the sorcery accusation as "pesant superstition" with a gruff and somewhat embarrassed wave. That was the end of that conversation. For my part, I read about history, anthropology, demographics, cosmology, and anything else that might clarify Haiti. Even though I didn't know Mme Providence, much less believe her capable of magical poisoning, I understood why such modes of explaining misfortune flourished in Haiti and even, to some extent, where they'd come from. Similar forms of accusation and symbolic reparation flourished across the plantation economies of the Caribbean and southern United States and parts of Latin America.[3] These attitudes, although they might be nonsense etiologically, made sense to me as a certain reflection of social conditions in rural Haiti.

Extending a hermeneutic of generosity to those who rely more on a hermeneutic of suspicion (like the suspicion to which Mme Providence was subjected) has been an enduring intellectual and personal project for me. Those first years in Haiti taught me to understand the force that sorcery allegations, and rumor and umbrage of all sorts, can have. Like the doctor's resignation, it was a response to being socialized for scarcity, to zero-sum solutions and diminishing returns. It was then that I began reading the work of Gutiérrez and others seeking to interpret not only scripture but its meaning in Latin American contexts. Recently, a fellow physician-anthropologist and friend asked me how Paul Ricoeur's work had informed my own passing commentary on hermeneutics. It was true that I'd slogged through three volumes of Ricoeur's book on time and narrative—in French no less—in graduate school. But that wasn't what hermeneutics meant for me. I saw it, in the spirit of Gutiérrez, as a much older endeavor, and one predicated on an ethical stance. What I learned from Gutiérrez above all was that hermeneutics was praxis. He'd taught me to look for the hermeneutics of hope that might follow the hermeneutics of generosity I'd sought to extend to my hosts.

Liberation theology continues to be, for me, an inexhaustible font of inspiration. I see the spirituality associated with it as, at the very least, aspirational: any of us can aspire to be better—but only if we seek to attack contemporary poverty and to remember that we live in one world, not three. Nothing that I've seen, from plague to famine to flood to quake, could persuade me otherwise.

*   *   *

Later, Gutiérrez himself inspired me. On one of my early trips to Lima in the early 1990s, the first person I wanted to meet, beyond my new hosts and patients in a squatter settlement north of Lima, was Father Gustavo. Although he did not know me, a newly minted gringo doctor, I came with a friend and colleague, Dr. Jaime Bayona, the founder of Socios En Salud, as Partners In Health is called in Peru, and with Dr. Jim Kim. I brought Father Gutiérrez copies of my first two books, works of medical anthropology that drew heavily on his thinking. He received us in Rímac, where he was a parish priest and running a center for study and reflection. It was a tough time in Peru: the tail end of a huge cholera epidemic, itself the tail end of a civil war. *Fujishock* was what our hosts termed the fiscal austerity programs of the government. There was ill will to spare. Our first project in the slums of Lima, a pharmacy for poor people, had just been blown up by a pipe bomb.

The core of Father Gustavo's teaching has always been that we must make a preferential option for the poor. I distill this teaching into three simple points: first, that *real service to the poor involves understanding global poverty.* (The converse is also sometimes true.)

Poverty is not some accident of nature but the result of historically given and economically driven forces. Human beings constitute the social world, and we will always shape it. Understanding poverty and inequality requires multiple disciplines: economics, ethics, law, sociology, anthropology, epidemiology, and so forth. Most of all, it requires listening to those most affected by poverty, which is to say the poor and otherwise marginalized. Listening is also a significant part of accompaniment, and of clinical medicine. Listening is thus both engagement and research. It would not be remiss to think of reverent listening as encompassing the four traditional pillars of Dominican life: prayer, study, service, and community. "Your desk is your prayer bench," as Dominic said. This academic, information-seeking approach is how option-for-the-poor medicine should work, too. If there is anything that distinguishes Partners In Health from other nongovernmental organizations, it is less an insistence on social justice—many organizations make similar claims—and more an insistence on linking our service work to training and to research. It is why our efforts are so often linked to a research university.

Father Gustavo's theology stems from a similar conviction, even though he wasn't always rewarded for it. Until less than a decade ago, he'd never had an academic appointment; his research and writing were additions to his priestly vocation. Yet this has not resulted in an intellectual profile that anyone would call amateurish. As Father Dan Groody puts it, "Gutiérrez would bring his claims of faith into dialogue with such thinkers as Albert Camus, G. W. F. Hegel, Jean-Paul Sartre, and Gabriel Marcel; film directors such as Luis Buñuel and Ingmar Bergman, and writers such as Peruvians José María Arguedas, Felipe Guaman Poma de Ayala, and César Vallejo."[4] Along the same lines, we succeeded, in 1995, in bringing Father Gustavo together with Noam Chomsky for a day-long, wide-ranging conversation. Somewhere, I hope, this conversation has been taped and archived.[5]

Second, *an understanding of poverty must be linked to efforts to end it*. Father Gustavo has often noted, in his writing and in his speaking, that poverty means death. Nowhere is this more evident than in medicine; and most medical specialists and institutions are aware of the need to do something about it. Imagine trying to do clinical research in an American teaching hospital without providing any clinical services. The study of poverty without an expressed concern with ending it is seen with a hermeneutic of suspicion by most of the people with whom I've lived and worked.

A preferential option for the poor informs our clinical work and also our efforts to move beyond individual patients to remedy inadequacies, inefficiencies, and gaps in health systems. To show how much we've been influenced by this and related notions, let me go back to 1987, when we founded Partners In Health. Our mission statement, duly filed with public authorities in order to start a public charity, reads as follows:

> Our mission is to provide a preferential option for the poor in health care. By establishing long-term relationships with sister organizations based in settings of poverty, Partners In Health strives to achieve two overarching goals: to bring the benefits of modern medical science to those most in need of them and to serve as an antidote to despair. We draw on the resources of the world's elite medical and academic institutions and on the lived experience of the world's poorest and sickest communities. We are dedicated to providing the highest level of clinical care possible while alleviating the crushing social and economic burden of poverty that creates obstacles to health. At its root, our mission is both medical and moral. It is based on solidarity, rather than charity alone. When our patients are ill and have no access to care, our team of health professionals, scholars, and activists will do whatever it takes to make them well—just as we would do if

a member of our own families—or we ourselves—were ill. We stand with our patients, some of the poorest and sickest victims of poverty and disease, in their struggle for equity and social justice.

In the intervening quarter of a century, our mission has spread to a dozen countries. But it's the same mission. Only the word "elite" has been dropped from our description of the institutions from which we channel resources. It was replaced with "academic."

Third, *as science and technology advance, our structural sin deepens.* This is no Tea-Party assertion; we love science and technology. It is just an observation to the effect that an increase in knowledge and power brings an increase in responsibility. As the effectiveness of medical interventions grows, our failure to use such interventions justly widens the "outcome gap."

Let me take cholera as an example. I have already mentioned Peru's cholera epidemic. The decades since that epidemic have brought new medical developments: new antibiotics, better formulations of oral rehydration salts, and new preventives, including safe vaccines. There have been new developments in water purification and sanitation, and new communications platforms have altered the way we report epidemics.

Despite these advances, in 2010 cholera appeared for the first time ever in Haiti, introduced inadvertently by a soldier from a region of the world where the disease is endemic. Cholera exploded like a bomb in Haiti, becoming the world's largest epidemic—both in absolute terms and proportionally. Yet with more than half a million sick and thousands dead, relief agencies still haggled over whether or not to use the vaccine, which was not available during the previous Latin American epidemic but has since gone through trials showing it to be safe.

The harm done by this twenty-first-century epidemic is worse in some ways than any of the larger ones that may have preceded it, for cholera is now, in contrast to nineteenth-century epidemics, a disease *exclusively* of the poor. In other words, the pathogen has made a far more radical preferential option for the poor than have those fighting it.

*   *   *

"Structural violence," "immodest claims of causality," and "a hermeneutic of generosity"—these concepts figure heavily in my written work, even when they are not called out by name. Far from suffering from the "anxiety of influence," I am proud of my debt to Gustavo Gutiérrez and to liberation theology.

Making a preferential option for the poor ought to be easy in medicine—just follow the pathology, and that's where it leads you—but it's not. There are a million traps, so many of them analytic, but the most cunningly laid traps are perhaps best termed spiritual ones: failures of imagination, failures to extend a hermeneutic of generosity (or suspicion) when warranted, failure to listen patiently, much less reverently. These failures afflict all of us, which is why, no doubt, all of Father Gustavo's work can be seen as spiritual. Father Groody put it this way in introducing Gutiérrez as a "spiritual master" when compared to many less humble proponents of liberation from poverty: "Beneath the theological words and the social analysis were attitudes of self-righteousness, judgmentalism, and aggressiveness that left me wanting to fight for liberation from a deeper place. I began to appreciate not only that one fights for liberation but how one does it. I was drawn particularly to those whose fight for justice emerged from a quality of soul and deep spirituality."[6]

One could paraphrase: the self-styled liberators from poverty are too often those who want to preach, rather than listen, to the poor. The theme of receptive hearing as linked to humility runs throughout Father Gutiérrez's work as both pastor and as a theologian. "Working in this world [of the poor] and becoming familiar with it, I came to realize, together with others, the first thing to do is to listen."[7] Gutiérrez wrote these words in 2009, but has instantiated them throughout his five decades as a priest and theologian. Listening might seem easy in a classroom at

Harvard or Notre Dame, or in a rectory in Rimac or in Rome. It isn't. Among the poor, especially those who are sick, it's hard and often painful.

My experiences in Mirebalais and elsewhere in Haiti, including those registered after the January 2010 earthquake, tried me in ways I would not have anticipated. Regarding Mme Providence, I was appalled that a woman could be publicly excoriated and worse for "eating" two children, but I was determined to understand how such explanatory models might come about. I tried not to turn away. I still work in Mirebalais, as do Ophelia Dahl and so many of our co-workers, including a new generation of physicians and nurses and a host of partners that has grown quickly since the earthquake. Soon we will open what will be Haiti's largest teaching hospital, not more than a few hundred yards from where the unfortunate Mme Providence was jailed and beaten. The prison still stands and has not been much improved over thirty years, as we discovered to our great shame when cholera ripped through it, killing several prisoners before we acted with sufficient force to end the epidemic behind bars.

As long as poverty and inequality persist, as long as people are wounded and imprisoned and despised, we humans will need accompaniment—practical, spiritual, intellectual. It is for this reason, and for many others, that I am grateful for Father Gustavo's presence on this wounded but beautiful earth.

Notes

[1] Mark Danner, "The Truth of El Mozote," *New Yorker*, December 6, 1993.

[2] See Johan Galtung, "Violence, Peace, and Peace Research," *Journal of Peace Research* 6, no. 3 (1969): 167–91.

[3] Alfred Métraux, *Haitian Voodoo,* trans. Hugo Charteris (New York: Schocken, 1972); Karen McCarthy Brown. "Systematic Remembering, Systematic Forgetting: Ogou in Haiti," in *Africa's Ogun: Old World and New,* ed. Sandra Barnes (Bloomington: Indiana University Press, 1989), esp. 67. See also Wade Davis, *Passage of Darkness: The Ethnobiology of the Haitian Zombie* (Chapel Hill: University of North Carolina Press, 1988); and Michael Taussig, *The Devil*

and Commodity Fetishism in South America (Chapel Hill: University of North Carolina Press, 1980).

[4] Daniel G. Groody, ed., *Gustavo Gutiérrez: Spiritual Writings* (Maryknoll, NY: Orbis Books, 2011), 24.

[5] I should add that it was concern for the poor, rather than some doctrinaire that brought Chomsky and Gutiérrez together, just as it motivates the work of Partners In Health and allied organizations. We have worked under a wide variety of economic systems (socialist, capitalist, kleptocratic, postsocialist, and others harder to classify) and have learned a lot about building health systems for the poor in wildly disparate settings. Scholarship and commentary, like medicine, benefit from a lessening of ideology and an increase in historical specificity and empirical efforts to improve delivery of services.

[6] Groody, ed., *Gustavo Gutiérrez,* 18

[7] Gustavo Gutiérrez, *The Density of the Present: Selected Writings* (Maryknoll, NY: Orbis Books, 1999), 171.

2

Saying and Showing to the Poor: "God Loves You"

Gustavo Gutiérrez

Theology and the Poor

Theology has, from the beginning, been in dialogue with both the practical and theoretical elements of contemporary life. In this way, we also each bring our personal and collective journey to the task of theology. For example, I do theology as one who comes from a context of deep poverty, and thus for me, the first question of theology is *how do we say to the poor: God loves you?* I understand that the words "God loves you" are not difficult to say. But this message—true as it is—presents a monumental challenge given the daily life of poor persons and their experience of exclusion and nonlove, of being forgotten, of having no social rights. Today, Paul Farmer and many others argue, "The poor have the right to have rights." Again, this is true but is not the reality for most. In fact, they do not have this "right to have rights." And so, what does it mean to take seriously the question of how to say and to show to persons living in the structure of violence, living in social injustice and seeming insignificance, that "God loves you?" *This is the question that the*

This text is based on public remarks at the University of Notre Dame on October 24, 2011, during a joint appearance with Dr. Paul Farmer at the symposium, "Re-Imagining Accompaniment: Global Health and Liberation Theology."

theology of liberation attempts to answer. The answer to this question takes us to the heart of the gospel, where we see the primacy of the poor in God's kingdom. And thus we address the poor not only to make life better for the poor but also to announce the gospel to the world. Liberation from the sin of social injustice and exclusion is thus a clear sign of evangelization and the reality of God's reign on earth.

In this way, theology is utterly practical, a reflection not merely on theories and concepts but on life as it really is and as it really can be. The various challenges to human life—economic, political, environmental, and medical—may seem disconnected from theology, but they are not. Theology is a reflection about life in light of the reality of God. And this means that theology is very historical. It develops in the history of the church as we try to announce the gospel within a concrete situation and in a way relevant for daily life. Thus theology is "in the middle," between the living faith of believers and the task of announcing that faith in the world. More specifically, this means that to be coherent, theology must pay attention to the situations in poor countries or the contexts of historically excluded groups in rich countries. Thus in the United States you have black theology, Hispanic theology, Asian American theology, feminist theology. In my part of the world, the suffering of poor persons gave rise to liberation theology. Though adapted to particular situations, this way of doing theology is not new. The Bible itself does not adopt a "view from nowhere," to use a current phrase. Jesus, of course, displays this par excellence, speaking from the perspective of the poor and the excluded, affirming God's special care for them.

One of the central axioms of liberation theology has thus been "the preferential option for the poor." Sometimes this concept is misinterpreted to mean that there is a competition for God's love between the rich and the poor. This is not the meaning. In fact, the concept displays the *universality* of God's love for all—a love that, in a world structured to the benefit of the powerful, extends *even* to the least among us. In fact, Jesus shows us that God's love is clearest there. Like a mother who tends most tenderly to the weakest and threatened of her children, so it is with God's care for the poor. And the call of the gospel is for us to do the same, to make the same option, to show that God's love is universal by focusing our attention on the most threatened among us. What the preferential option for the poor reveals is that the calculus of the gospel is not the same as our world's. In present structures, attention is given first to the powerful and wealthy, with the poor receiving, perhaps, the leftovers. This is far from universal love. But only when we opt preferentially for the poorest and weakest can we even begin to display universality— anything less is tainted with the exclusive ways of present social structures. But God's way—placing the poor first among all— makes clear to us how un-universal our love often is.

When we speak about the preferential option for the poor, we must be very conscious about the practical dimensions, too. Here I refer to the causes of poverty. For a long time, poverty was understood as a fate: some people are born poor, other people are born rich, and both must accept this fate. To be sure, the duty of the rich was to be generous, but the underlying structure was not questioned. The assumption was that, for some, poverty is the will of God. We cannot accept this. Indeed, to be for the poor is not to accept their poverty. In liberation theology, we ask how it could be possible to be committed to the poor if we are not against poverty. As Dr. Farmer knows better than most, poverty for billions on this planet means an early death. We need to be clear, then, that poverty is an evil. I think of a hero, for both Paul and me, like Bartolomé de las Casas, the great opponent of the sixteenth-century Spanish Conquest of the Americas. He reported back to Spain that "the Indians are dying before their time." What las Casas's phrase emphasizes is that the early death of the poor is not God's will but a rejection of it. To speak of the poor, thus, without opposing the poverty that kills them, is a major obstacle to announcing the gospel. One of the key motives of liberation theology is simply to make sure that this mistake—idealizing the poor and accepting early death as their fate—is not made in the church.

Liberation Theology and the
Work of Partners In Health

Dr. Farmer commented to me in Peru that diseases make their own preferential option for the poor. Certainly this was true in my beloved country, especially with outbreaks of tuberculosis and cholera in the 1980s. Capitalizing on a lack of access to sanitation, to good food and nutrition, and to basic health care, diseases are most at home in the midst of grinding poverty. But this too is where Dr. Farmer and Partners In Health make their home—as they did among my people in Peru. And they are not simply delivering medicine, but practicing accompaniment. To be sure, something very unique about Partners In Health is their ability to put the world's highest level of medical care at the service of the poor. But their presence among the sick poor is transformative too. Illness brings with it great sufferings—not the least of which is an early death. And as the poor are "dying before their time," they also often live and die without influence and social significance. Consider Haiti, the poorest country on the continent. Its habitants have a long history of suffering and early death, yet Paul and his colleagues have helped this people display their strengths and capacities. Most of the massive Partners In Health team in Haiti is composed of Haitians, becoming architects of their own God-given dignity and future. They, the poor, are themselves making the option for the poor.

For Partners In Health, the goal in places like Haiti is to accompany people in their suffering and to seek the changes necessary to remedy their suffering and the entire situation that has given rise to their suffering. The focus is thus health in its broadest meaning in every dimension of human existence. And the comprehensive nature of their work shows us that the early death, which so often comes with poverty, is not a misfortune but an injustice. We as a human community are making poverty, and we can change that situation, too. The causes of poverty are obviously complex, and poor countries, as Paul has so often said, must take their own share of responsibility. But because we know that it is possible globally to create systems of health and development, we also know that systemic poverty is not an accident or a fate. Correcting the injustice of poverty must involve both accompaniment of the locally poor and advocacy of the globally powerful —the twin tasks that Dr. Farmer undertakes by his very nature.

I also wish to place the work of Partners In Health in theological perspective. I find that the way they approach accompaniment of the poor has deep resonance with the message of the gospel. Jesus bears witness to the Kingdom of God through his words and deeds—and the healing of the sick has a prominent role in his work. Jesus healed the leper, the paralyzed, the blind, the deaf, and many others who suffer diseases. All of this was a message of life, as the Acts of the Apostles says: Jesus passed through this world "doing good" (Acts 10:38). And Jesus not only healed the sick, but he allowed the sick to participate in their own healing; very often Jesus told them: "Your faith has saved you." Once healed, they too became agents of healing and were invited to be agents of their own destiny. In all of this, we see that Jesus directed his message, first and foremost, to the poorest of society—"the last shall be first"—and from them to all the people. This structured approach, beginning with accompaniment of the poor and moving outward to a global invitation to all people, is also found in Paul's vision and in the work of Partners In Health.

Spirituality and the Preferential Option for the Poor

I know that Dr. Farmer is a bit shy and reluctant to expound on theology and spirituality, but in fact his practice speaks very much to this matter. As I stated above, Christian theology must be grounded in the reality of human suffering and exclusion if it is to be at the service of discipleship and transformation. And the practice of discipleship—"sequela Christi," *following Jesus*—is precisely the traditional definition for Christian spirituality. Spirituality is not some immaterial realm pertaining to our soul but not our body, to our beliefs but not our actions. *Rather, our spirituality is the comprehensive way in which we live out our faith.* Spirituality moves in the field of praxis: there is no faith if there are no works (Jas 2:17). And in this way we see that accompaniment of the poor—so central to the message of the gospel—must always be a reference point for our primary task: following Jesus. This, of course, does not mean that we all must care for the poor in the same way and to the same extent. It is true that the "option" for the poor is not optional; it is a demand made of all Christians. But people are diverse, with many different characteristics, possibilities, and capacities. Thus there are "mil maneras," a thousand ways to practice the preferential option for the poor. Finding our own way is the task of our discernment and the goal of our spirituality. What must be clear, though, is that to follow Jesus implies priority for the poor.

I want to emphasize that the preferential option for the poor is not made because the poor are somehow better than others, more virtuous or noble. Idealizing the poor would be the wrong basis for the spirituality we are describing. Often the poor are quite generous and beautiful people, but sometimes not. Nor are our motives for aiding the poor always pure; there can be a temptation to self-congratulation and ego-boosts in this work. So in our spirituality it is supremely important that each of us refines the basis of our preferential option for the poor to say: I accompany them not because they are all good, or because I am all good, but because God is good. The ongoing discernment necessary to see that this is a theocentric option—centered in God's love and life—is particularly suited to habits of communal and personal prayer, practices so central to Christian spirituality.

One of the fruits of prayerful reflection on our life's work is that we all come to see the ways in which we are poor. And here we see in Christian spirituality the multiple meanings of poverty. Pope Benedict XVI made this point during a visit he made to Latin America. He said, "The preferential option for the poor is implicit in the Christological faith in the God who became poor for us, so as to enrich us with his poverty (cf. 2 Cor 8:9)." We see here reference to the way in which we are called to be, as Jesus recommends, "poor in spirit." This kind of poverty has been likened to childhood, a stance of trust and dependence on God as the source of our life. Even an adult who is over seventy—or in my case over eighty—can be a spiritual child and place our lives in the hands of God. And this personal poverty of spirit is an important resource—an enrichment, in Benedict's sense—in making the preferential option for the materially poor, because we become aware that the love of God is universal. Nobody is outside of it; nobody is a nobody. As we see in the Bible, this love is directed in the first place to the most abandoned and mistreated. But the preference is not opposed to universality: the gospel of Jesus signals priorities, not exclusions.

The reason why spirituality is so connected to accompaniment of those battling material poverty—suffering the death of sickness and of social insignificance—is that Christians consider the creation of the world as a gift of life. And poverty is against the meaning of that gift, contrary to the goal of creation and the meaning of life. Jesus said, "I am the way, the truth, and *the life*" (Jn 14:6). Poverty is a threat to this life. We are not really in solidarity with the poor if we are not against poverty. You do not need to read liberation theology to see that. But the truth of this claim is a call to rethink many things, including how we do theology. In the first place, though, the need for solidarity in the face of scandalous poverty is a call to praxis, action informed by placing our best intellects and most skilled attention at its service. For Christians, the manifold challenges and opportunities of the preferential option for the poor thus should constitute a central component of our spirituality. And here the key action that provides the spiritual dynamism of this tall task is close friendship with God and with others, especially those who suffer.

I began by suggesting, as a theologian, that my aim should be to help the church answer the question of how we can say to the poor "God loves you." I do believe that this is a central task of theology, but I am not self-important enough to think that we theologians provide very good answers to this question. And we all have our limitations. For the last fifty years, I have been a theologian—but only in my free moments. Now, at Notre Dame, I have a chance to spend some more time on scholarship, but in my life theology has always been in the middle: between the sufferings and hopes of the people with whom I live. And because in my life I have known and seen so much poverty, and how it robs the poor of the health and life that God has intended for them, I am so deeply aware that good theology alone cannot meet the challenge. What is needed is a comprehensive commitment to building a just world. And I think that the experience of Paul and the thousands with whom he works—all of them propelled by friendship—shows that it will take the efforts of each of us, in our "thousand ways," to continue to say and show to the poor, "God loves you."

3

Health, Healing, and Social Justice

Insights from Liberation Theology

Paul Farmer

If I define my neighbor as the one I must go out to look for, on the highways and byways, in the factories and slums, on the farms and in the mines—then my world changes. This is what is happening with the "option for the poor," for in the gospel it is the poor person who is the neighbor par excellence. . . .

But the poor person does not exist as an inescapable fact of destiny. His or her existence is not politically neutral, and it is not ethically innocent. The poor are a by-product of the system in which we live and for which we are responsible. They are marginalized by our social and cultural world. They are the oppressed, exploited proletariat, robbed of the fruit of their labor and despoiled of their humanity. Hence the poverty of the poor is not a call to generous relief action, but a demand that we go and build a different social order.

—*Gustavo Gutiérrez,*
The Power of the Poor in History

This chapter is reprinted from Paul Farmer, *Pathologies of Power: Health, Human Rights, and the New War on the Poor* (Berkeley: University of California Press, 2003).

Not everything that the poor are and do is gospel. But a great deal of it is.

—*Jon Sobrino,*
Spirituality of Liberation

Making a Preferential
Option for the Poor

For decades now, proponents of liberation theology have argued that people of faith must make a "preferential option for the poor." As discussed by Brazil's Leonardo Boff, a leading contributor to the movement, "the Church's option is a preferential option for the poor, against their poverty." The poor, Boff adds, "are those who suffer injustice. Their poverty is produced by mechanisms of impoverishment and exploitation. Their poverty is therefore an evil and an injustice."[1] To those concerned with health, a preferential option for the poor offers both a challenge and an insight. It challenges doctors and other health providers to make an option—a choice—for the poor, to work on their behalf.

The insight is, in a sense, an epidemiological one: most often, diseases themselves make a preferential option for the poor. Every careful survey, across boundaries of time and space, shows us that the poor are sicker than the nonpoor. They're at increased risk of dying prematurely, whether from increased exposure to pathogens (including pathogenic situations) or from decreased access to services—or, as is most often the case, from both of these "risk factors" working together.[2] Given this indisputable association, medicine has a clear—if not always observed—mandate to devote itself to populations struggling against poverty.

It's also clear that many health professionals feel paralyzed by the magnitude of the challenge. Where on earth does one start? We have received endless, detailed prescriptions from experts, many of them manifestly dismissive of initiatives coming from afflicted communities themselves. But those who formulate health policy in Geneva, Washington, New York, or Paris do not really labor to transform the social conditions of the wretched of the earth. Instead, the actions of technocrats—and what physician is not a technocrat?—are most often tantamount to *managing* social inequality, to keeping the problem under control. The limitations of such tinkering are sharp, as Peruvian theologian Gustavo Gutiérrez warns:

> Latin American misery and injustice go too deep to be responsive to palliatives. Hence we speak of social revolution, not reform; of liberation, not development; of socialism, not modernization of the prevailing system. "Realists" call these statements romantic and utopian. And they should, for the reality of these statements is of a kind quite unfamiliar to them.[3]

Liberation theology, in contrast to officialdom, argues that genuine change will be most often rooted in small communities of poor people; and it advances a simple methodology— *observe, judge, act.*[4] Throughout Latin America, such base-community movements have worked to take stock of their situations and devise strategies for change.[5] The approach is straight-forward. Although it has been termed "simplistic" by technocrats and experts, this methodology has proven useful for promoting health in settings as diverse as Brazil, Guatemala, El Salvador, rural Mexico, and urban Peru. Insights from liberation theology have proven useful in rural Haiti too, perhaps the sickest region of the hemisphere and the one I know best. With all due respect for health policy expertise, then, this chapter explores the implications—so far, almost completely overlooked—of liberation theology for medicine and health policy.[6]

Observe, judge, act. The "observe" part of the formula implies analysis. There has been no shortage of analysis from the self-appointed apostles of international health policy, who insist that their latest recipes become the cornerstones of health policy in all of Latin America's nations.[7] Within ministries of health, one quickly learns not to question these fads, since failure to acknowledge the primacy of the regnant health ideology can stop many projects from ever getting off the ground. But other, less conventional sources of analysis are relevant to our understanding of health and illness. It's surprising that many Catholic bishops of Latin America, for centuries allied with the elites of their countries, have in more recent decades chosen to favor tough-minded social analysis of their societies. Many would argue that liberation theology's key documents were hammered out at the bishops' conventions in Medellín in 1968 and in Puebla in 1978. In both instances, progressive bishops, working with like-minded theologians, denounced the political and economic forces that immiserate so many Latin Americans. Regarding causality, the bishops did not mince words:

> Let us recall once again that the present moment in the history of our peoples is characterized in the social order, and from an objective point of view, by a situation of underdevelopment. Certain phenomena point an accusing finger at it: marginalized existence, alienation, and poverty. In the last analysis it is conditioned by structures of economic, political, and cultural dependence on the great industrialized metropolises, the latter enjoying a monopoly on technology and science (neocolonialism).[8]

What began timidly in the preparation for the Medellín meeting in 1968 was by 1978 a strong current. "The Puebla document," remarks Boff, "moves immediately to the structural analysis of these forces and denounces the systems, structures, and mechanisms that 'create a situation where the rich get richer at the expense of the poor, who get even poorer.'"[9] In both of these meetings, the bishops were at pains to argue that "this reality calls for personal conversion and profound structural changes that will meet the legitimate aspirations of the people for authentic social justice."[10]

Liberation theology has always been about the struggle for social and economic rights. The injunction to "observe" leads to descriptions of the conditions of the Latin American poor, and also to claims regarding the origins of these conditions. These causal claims have obvious implications for a rethinking of human rights, as Gutiérrez explains:

> A structural analysis better suited to Latin American reality has led certain Christians to speak of the "rights of the poor" and to interpret the defense of human rights under this new formality. The adjustment is not merely a matter of words. This alternative language represents a critical approach to the laissez-faire, liberal doctrine to the effect that our society enjoys an equality that in fact does not exist. This new formulation likewise seeks constantly to remind us of what is really at stake in the defense of human rights: the misery and spoliation of the poorest of the poor, the conflictive character of Latin American life and society, and the biblical roots of the defense of the poor.[11]

Liberation theologians are among the few who have dared to underline, from the left, the deficiencies of the liberal human rights movement. The most glaring of these deficiencies emerges from intimate acquaintance with the suffering of the poor in countries that are signatory to all modern human rights agreements. When children living in poverty die of measles, gastroenteritis, and malnutrition, and yet no party is judged guilty of a human rights violation, liberation theology finds fault with the entire notion of human rights as defined within liberal democracies. Thus, even before judgment is rendered, the "observe" part of the formula reveals atrocious conditions as atrocious.

The "judge" part of the equation is nonetheless important even if it is, in a sense, pre-judged. We look at the lives of the poor and are sure, just as they are, that something is terribly wrong. They are targets of structural violence. (Some of the bishops

termed this "structural sin.")[12] This is, granted, an a priori judgment
—but it is seldom incorrect, for analysis of social suffering invariably reveals its social origins. It is not primarily cataclysms of
nature that wreak havoc in the lives of the Latin American poor:

> All these aspects which make up the overall picture of the
> state of humanity in the late twentieth century have one
> common name: oppression. They all, including the hun-
> ger suffered by millions of human beings, result from the
> oppression of some human beings by others. The impo-
> tence of international bodies in the face of generally rec-
> ognized problems, their inability to effect solutions, stems
> from the self-interest of those who stand to benefit from
> their oppression of other human beings. In each major
> problem there is broad recognition of both the moral
> intolerableness and the political nonviability of the existing
> situation, coupled with a lack of capacity to respond. If the
> problem is (or the problems are) a conflict of interests, then
> the energy to find the solution can come only from the
> oppressed themselves.[13]

Rendering judgment based on careful observation can be
a powerful experience. The Brazilian sociologist Paulo Freire
coined the term *conscientization*, or "consciousness raising," to
explain the process of coming to understand how social structures cause injustice.[14] This "involves discovering that evil not
only is present in the hearts of powerful individuals who muck
things up for the rest of us but is embedded in the very structures
of society, so that those structures, and not just individuals who
work within them, must be changed if the world is to change."[15]
Liberation theology uses the primary tools of social analysis to
reveal the mechanisms by which social structures cause social
misery. Such analysis, unlike many fraudulently dispassionate academic treatises, is meant to challenge the observer to judge. It
requires a very different approach than that most often used by,

say, global health bureaucrats. It requires an approach that implicates the observer, as Jon Sobrino notes:

> The reality posed by the poor, then, is no rhetorical question. Precisely as sin, this reality tends to conceal itself, to be relativized, to pass itself off as something secondary and provisional in the larger picture of human achievements. It is a reality that calls men and women not only to recognize and acknowledge it, but to take a primary, basic position regarding it. Outwardly, this reality demands that it be stated for what it is, and denounced. . . . But inwardly, this same reality is a question for human beings as themselves participants in the sin of humankind. . . . The poor of the world are not the causal products of human history. No, poverty results from the actions of other human beings.[16]

How is all of this relevant to medicine? It is more realistic, surely, to ask how this could be considered irrelevant to medicine. In the wealthy countries of the Northern Hemisphere, the relatively poor often travel far and wait long for health care inferior to that available to the wealthy. In the third world, where conservative estimates suggest that one billion souls live in dire poverty, the plight of the poor is even worse. How do they cope? They don't, often enough. The poor there have short life expectancies, often dying of preventable or treatable diseases or from accidents. Few have access to modern medical care. In fact, most of the third world poor receive no effective biomedical care at all. For some people, there is no such thing as a measles vaccine. For many, tuberculosis is as lethal as AIDS. Childbirth involves mortal risk. In an age of explosive development in the realm of medical technology, it is unnerving to find that the discoveries of Salk, Sabin, and even Pasteur remain irrelevant to much of humanity.

Many physicians are uncomfortable acknowledging these harsh facts of life and death. To do so, one must admit that the majority of premature deaths are, as the Haitians would say, "stupid deaths." They are completely preventable with the tools already available to the fortunate few. By the criteria of liberation theology, these deaths are a great injustice and a stain on the conscience of modem medicine and science. Why, then, are these premature deaths not the primary object of discussion and debate within our professional circles? Again, liberation theology helps to answer this question. First, acknowledging the scandalous conditions of those living in poverty often requires a rejection of comforting relativism. Sobrino is addressing fellow theologians, but what he writes is of relevance to physicians, too:

> In order to recognize the truth of creation today, one must take another tack in this first, basic moment, a moment of honesty. The data, the statistics, may seem cold. They may seem to have precious little to do with theology. But we must take account of them. This is where we have to start. "Humanity" today is the victim of poverty and institutionalized violence. Often enough this means death, slow or sudden.[17]

A second reason that premature deaths are not the primary topic of our professional discussion is that the viewpoints of poor people will inevitably be suppressed or neglected as long as elites control most means of communication. Thus the steps of observation and judgment are usually difficult, because vested interests, including those controlling "development" and even international health policy, have an obvious stake in shaping observations about causality and in attenuating harsh judgments of harsh conditions. (This is, of course, another reason that people living in poverty are cited in this book as experts on structural violence and human rights.)

Finally, the liberation theologians and the communities from which they draw their inspiration agree that it is necessary to *act* on these reflections. The "act" part of the formula implies much more than reporting one's findings. The goal of this judging is not producing more publications or securing tenure in a university: "In order to *understand* the world, Latin American Christians are taking seriously the insights of social scientists, sociologists, and economists, in order to learn how to *change* the world."[18] Sobrino puts it this way: "There is no doubt that the only correct way to love the poor will be to struggle for their liberation. This liberation will consist, first and foremost, in their liberation at the most elementary level—that of their simple, physical life, which is what is at stake in the present situation."[19] I could confirm his assessment with my own experiences in Haiti and elsewhere, including the streets of some of the cities of this hemisphere's most affluent country. What's at stake, for many of the poor, is physical survival.

The results of following this "simple" methodology can be quiet and yet effective, as in the small-scale project described in the next section. But careful reflection on the inhuman conditions endured by so many in this time of great affluence can of course also lead to more explosive actions. Retrospective analysis of these explosions often reveals them to be last-ditch efforts to escape untenable situations. That is, the explosions follow innumerable peaceful attempts to attenuate structural violence and the lies that help sustain it. The Zapatistas, who refer often to early death from treatable illnesses, explain it this way in an early communiqué:

> Some ask why we decided to begin now, if we were prepared before. The answer is that before this we tried other peaceful and legal roads to change, but without success. During these last ten years more than 150,000 of our indigenous brothers and sisters have died from curable diseases. The federal, state, and municipal governments' economic and social plans do not even consider any real solution to our problems, and consist of giving us handouts at election times. But these crumbs of charity solve our problems for no more than a moment, and then,

death returns to our houses. That is why we think no, no more, enough of this dying useless deaths, it would be better to fight for change. If we die now, we will not die with shame, but with the dignity of our ancestors. Another 150,000 of us are ready to die if that is what is needed to waken our people from their deceit-induced stupor.[20]

Applying Principles of Liberation Theology to Medicine

To act as a physician in the service of poor or otherwise oppressed people is to prevent, whenever possible, the diseases that afflict them—but also to treat and, if possible, to cure. So where's the innovation in that? How would a health intervention inspired by liberation theology be different from one with more conventional underpinnings? Partners In Health has joined local community health activists to provide basic primary care and preventive services to poor communities in Mexico, Peru, the United States, and, especially, Haiti—offering what we have termed "pragmatic solidarity." Pragmatic solidarity is different from but nourished by solidarity per se, the desire to make common cause with those in need. Solidarity is a precious thing: people enduring great hardship often remark that they are grateful for the prayers and good wishes of fellow human beings. But when sentiment is accompanied by the goods and services that might diminish unjust hardship, surely it is enriched. To those in great need, solidarity without the pragmatic component can seem like so much abstract piety.

Lest all this talk of structural violence and explosive responses to it seem vague and far removed from the everyday obligations of medicine, allow me to give examples from my own clinical experience. How does liberation theology inform medical practice in, say, rural Haiti? Take tuberculosis, along with HIV the leading infectious cause of preventable adult deaths in the world. How might one observe, judge, and act in pragmatic solidarity with those most likely to acquire tuberculosis or already suffering from it?

The "observation" part of the formula is key, for it involves careful review of a large body of literature that seeks to explain the distribution of the disease within populations, to explore its clinical characteristics, and to evaluate tuberculosis treatment regimens. This sort of review is standard in all responsible health planning, but liberation theology would push analysis in two directions: first, to seek the root causes of the problem; second, *to elicit the experiences and views of poor people* and to incorporate these views into all observations, judgments, and actions.

Ironically enough, some who understand, quite correctly, that the underlying causes of tuberculosis are poverty and social inequality make a terrible error by failing to honor the experience and views of the poor in designing strategies to respond to the disease. What happens if, after analysis reveals poverty as the root cause of tuberculosis, tuberculosis control strategies ignore the sick and focus solely on eradicating poverty? Elsewhere, I have called this the "Luddite trap," since this ostensibly progressive view would have us ignore both current distress and the tools of modern medicine that might relieve it, thereby committing a new and grave injustice.[21] The destitute sick ardently desire the eradication of poverty, but their tuberculosis can be readily cured by drugs such as isoniazid and rifampin. The prescription for poverty is not so clear.

Careful review of the biomedical and epidemiological literature on tuberculosis does permit certain conclusions. One of the clearest is that the incidence of the disease is not at all random. Certainly, tuberculosis has claimed victims among the great (Frédéric Chopin, Fyodor Dostoyevsky, George Orwell, Eleanor Roosevelt), but historically it is a disease that has ravaged the economically disadvantaged.[22] This is especially true in recent decades: with the development of effective therapy in the mid-twentieth century came high cure rates—over 95 percent—for those with access to the right drugs for the right amount of time. Thus tuberculosis *deaths* now—which each year number in the millions—occur almost exclusively among the poor, whether they reside in the inner cities of the United States or in the poor countries of the Southern Hemisphere.[23]

The latest twists to the story—the resurgence of tuberculosis in the United States, the advent of HIV-related tuberculosis, and the development of strains of tuberculosis resistant to the first-line therapies developed in recent decades—serve to reinforce the thesis that *Mycobacterium tuberculosis*, the causative organism, makes its own preferential option for the poor.[24]

What "judgment" might be offered on these epidemiological and clinical facts? Many would find it scandalous that one of the world's leading causes of preventable adult deaths is a disease that, with the possible exception of emerging resistant strains, is more than 95 percent curable, with inexpensive therapies developed decades ago. Those inspired by liberation theology would certainly express distaste for a disease so partial to poor and debilitated hosts and would judge unacceptable the lack of therapy for those most likely to become ill with tuberculosis: poverty puts people at risk of tuberculosis and then bars them from access to effective treatment. An option-for-the-poor approach to tuberculosis would make the disease a top priority for research and development of new drugs and vaccines and at the same time would make programs to detect and cure all cases a global priority.

Contrast this reading to the received wisdom—and the current agenda—concerning tuberculosis. Authorities rarely blame the recrudescence of tuberculosis on the inequalities that structure our society. Instead, we hear mostly about biological factors (the advent of HIV, the mutations that lead to drug resistance) or about cultural and psychological barriers that result in "noncompliance." Through these two sets of explanatory mechanisms, one can expediently attribute high rates of treatment failure either to the organism or to uncooperative patients.

There are costs to seeing the problem in this way. If we see the resurgence or persistence of tuberculosis as an exclusively biological phenomenon, then we will shunt available resources to basic biological research, which, though needed, is not the primary solution, since almost all tuberculosis deaths result from lack of access to existing effective therapy. If we see the problem primarily as one of patient noncompliance, then we must necessarily ground our strategies in plans to change the patients rather than to change the weak tuberculosis control programs that fail to detect and cure the majority of cases. In either event, weak analysis produces the sort of dithering that characterizes current global tuberculosis policy, which must accept as its primary rebuke the shameful death toll that continues unabated.

How about the "act" part of the formula advocated by liberation theology? In a sense, it's simple: heal the sick. Prompt diagnosis and cure of tuberculosis are also the means to prevent new infections, so prevention and treatment are intimately linked. Most studies of tuberculosis in Haiti reveal that the vast majority of patients do not complete treatment—which explains why, until very recently, tuberculosis remained the leading cause of adult death in rural regions of Haiti. (It has now been surpassed by HIV.) But it does not need to be so. In the country's Central Plateau, Partners In Health worked with our sister organization, Zanmi Lasante, to devise a tuberculosis treatment effort that borrows a number of ideas—and also some passion—from liberation theology.

Although the Zanmi Lasante staff had, from the outset, identified and referred patients with pulmonary tuberculosis to its clinic, it gradually became clear that detection of new cases did not always lead to cure, even though all tuberculosis care, including medication, was free of charge. In December 1988, following the deaths from tuberculosis of three HIV-negative patients, all adults in their forties, the staff met to reconsider the care these individuals had received. How had the staff failed to prevent these deaths? How could we better observe, judge, and act as a community making common cause with the destitute sick?

Initially, we responded to these questions in differing ways. In fact, the early discussions were heated, with a fairly sharp divide between community health workers, who shared the social conditions of the patients, and the doctors and nurses, who did not. Some community health workers believed that tuberculosis patients with poor outcomes were the most economically im-poverished and thus the sickest; others hypothesized that patients lost interest in chemotherapy after ridding themselves of the symptoms that had caused them to seek medical advice. Feel-ing better, they returned as quickly as possible to the herculean task of providing for their families. Still others, including the physicians and nurses, attributed poor compliance to widespread beliefs that tuberculosis was a disorder inflicted through sorcery, beliefs that led patients to abandon biomedical therapy. A desire to focus blame on the patients' ignorance or misunderstanding was palpable, even though the physicians and nurses sought to cure the disease as ardently as anyone else involved in the program.

The caregivers' ideas about the causes of poor outcomes tended to coalesce in two directions: a *cognitivist-personalistic* pole that emphasized individual patient agency (curiously, "cultural" explanations fit best under this rubric, since beliefs about sorcery allegedly led patients to abandon therapy) and a *structural* pole that emphasized the patients' poverty. And this poverty, though generic to outsiders like the physicians from Port-au-Prince, had a vivid history to those from the region. Most of our tuberculosis patients were landless peasants living in the most dire poverty. They had lost their land a generation before when the Péli-gre Dam, part of an internationally funded development project, flooded their fertile valley.[25]

More meetings followed. Over the next several months, we devised a plan to improve services to patients with tuberculosis—and to test these discrepant hypotheses. Briefly, the new program set goals of detecting cases, supplying adequate chemotherapy, and providing close follow-up. Although they also continued contact screening and vaccination for infants, the staff of Zanmi Lasante was then most concerned with caring for smear-positive and coughing patients—believed to be the most important source of community exposure. The new program was aggressive and community-based, relying heavily on community health workers for close follow-up. It also responded to patients' appeals for nutritional assistance. The patients argued, often with some vehemence and always with eloquence, that to give medicines without food was tantamount to *lave men, siye atè* (washing one's hands and then wiping them dry in the dirt). Those diagnosed with tuberculosis who participated in the new treatment program were to receive daily visits from their village health worker during the first month following diagnosis. They would also receive financial aid of thirty dollars per month for the first three months; would be eligible for nutritional supplements; would receive regular reminders from their village health worker to attend the clinic; and would receive a five-dollar honorarium to defray "travel expenses" (for example, renting a donkey) for attending the clinic. If a patient did not attend, someone from the clinic—often a physician or an auxiliary nurse—would make a visit to the no-show's house. A series of forms, including a detailed initial interview schedule and home visit reports, regularized these arrangements and replaced the relatively limited forms used for other clinic patients.

Between February 1989 and September 1990, fifty patients were enrolled in the program. During the same period, the clinical staff diagnosed pulmonary tuberculosis in 213 patients from outside our catchment area. The first fifty of these patients to be diagnosed formed the comparison group that would be used to judge the efficacy of the new intervention. They were a "control group" only in the sense that they did not benefit from the community-based services and financial aid; all tuberculosis patients continued to receive free care.

The difference in the outcomes of the two groups was little short of startling. By June 1991, forty-six of the patients receiving the "enhanced package" were free of all symptoms, and none of those with symptoms met radiologic or clinical diagnostic criteria for persistent tuberculosis. Therefore, the medical staff concluded

that none had active pulmonary tuberculosis, giving the partici-
pants a cure rate of 100 percent. We could not locate all fifty of
the patients from outside the catchment area, but for the forty
patients examined more than one year after diagnosis, the cure
rate was barely half that of the first group, based on clinical,
laboratory, and radiographic evaluation. It should be noted that
this dismal cure rate was nonetheless higher than that reported
in most studies of tuberculosis outcomes in Haiti.[26]

Could this striking difference in outcome be attributed to
patients' ideas and beliefs about tuberculosis? Previous ethnographic research had revealed extremely complex and changing
ways of understanding and speaking about tuberculosis among
rural Haitians.[27] Because most physicians and nurses (and a few
community health workers) had hypothesized that patients who
"believed in sorcery" as a cause of tuberculosis would have higher rates of noncompliance with their medical regimens, we took
some pains to address this issue with each patient. As the resident
medical anthropologist, I conducted long—often very long—and
open-ended interviews with all patients in both groups, trying
to delineate the dominant explanatory models that shaped their
views of the disease. I learned that few from either group would
deny the possibility of sorcery as an etiologic factor in their own
illness, but I could discern no relationship between avowal of
such beliefs and compliance with a biomedical regimen. That is,
the outcomes were related to the quality of the program rather
than the quality of the patients' ideas about the disease. Suffice
it to say, this was not the outcome envisioned by many of my
colleagues in anthropology.

Although anthropologists are expected to underline the
importance of culture in determining the efficacy of efforts
to combat disease, in Haiti we learned that many of the most
important variables—initial exposure to infection, reactivation
of quiescent tuberculosis, transmission to household members,
access to diagnosis and therapy, length of convalescence, development of drug resistance, degree of lung destruction, and, most

of all, mortality—are all strongly influenced by economic factors. We concluded that removing structural barriers to "compliance," when coupled with financial aid, dramatically improved outcomes in poor Haitians with tuberculosis. This conclusion proved that the community health workers, and not the doctors, had been correct.

This insight forever altered approaches to tuberculosis within our program. It cut straight to the heart of the compliance question. Certainly, patients may be noncompliant, but how relevant is the notion of compliance in rural Haiti? Doctors may instruct their patients to eat well. But the patients will "refuse" if they have no food. They may be told to sleep in an open room and away from others, and here again they will be "noncompliant" if they do not expand and remodel their miserable huts. They may be instructed to go to a hospital. But if hospital care must be paid for in cash, as is the case throughout Haiti, and the patients have no cash, they will be deemed "grossly negligent." In a study published in collaboration with the Zanmi Lasante team, we concluded that "the hoary truth that poverty and tuberculosis are greater than the sum of their parts is once again supported by data, this time coming from rural Haiti and reminding us that such deadly synergism, formerly linked chiefly to crowded cities, is in fact most closely associated with deep poverty."[28]

Similar scenarios could be offered for diseases ranging from typhoid to AIDS. In each case, poor people are at higher risk of contracting the disease and are also less likely to have access to care. And in each case, analysis of the problem can lead researchers to focus on the patients' shortcomings (for example, failure to drink pure water, failure to use condoms, ignorance about public health and hygiene) or, instead, to focus on the conditions that structure people's risk (for example, lack of access to potable water, lack of economic opportunities for women, unfair distribution of the world's resources). In many current discussions of these plagues of the poor, one can discern a cognitivist-personalistic pole and a structural pole. Although focus on the

former is the current fashion, one of the chief benefits of the
latter mode of analysis is that it encourages physicians (and others
concerned to protect or promote health) to make common cause
with people who are both poor and sick.

A Social Justice Approach to
Addressing Disease and Suffering

Tuberculosis aside, what follows next from a perspective on
medicine that is based in liberation theology? Does recourse to
these ideas demand loyalty to any specific ideology? For me,
applying an option for the poor has never implied advancing
a particular strategy for a national economy. It does not imply preferring one form of development, or social system, over
another—although some economic systems are patently more
pathogenic than others and should be denounced as such by
physicians. Recourse to the central ideas of liberation theology
does not necessarily imply subscription to a specific body of
religious beliefs; Partners In Health and its sister organizations in
Haiti and Peru are completely ecumenical.[29] At the same time,
the flabby moral relativism of our times would have us believe
that we may now choose from a broad menu of approaches to
delivering effective health care services to the poor. This is simply
not true. Whether you are sitting in a clinic in rural Haiti, and
thus a witness to stupid deaths from infection, or sitting in an
emergency room in a US city, and thus the provider of first resort for forty million uninsured, you must acknowledge that the
commodification of medicine invariably punishes the vulnerable.

A truly committed quest for high-quality care for the destitute sick starts from the perspective that health is a fundamental human right. In contrast, commodified medicine invariably
begins with the notion that health is a desirable outcome to be
attained through the purchase of the right goods and services.
Socialized medicine in industrialized countries is no doubt a
step up from a situation in which market forces determine who

has access to care. But a perspective based in liberation theology highlights the fundamental weakness of this and other strategies of the affluent: if the governments of Scandinavian countries and that of France, for example, then spend a great deal of effort barring noncitizens from access to health care services, they will find few critics within their borders. (Indeed, the social democracies share a mania for border control.) But we will criticize them, and bitterly, because access to the fruits of science and medicine should not be determined by passports, but rather by need. The "health care for all" movement in the United States will never be morally robust until it truly means "all."

Liberation theology's first lesson for medicine is similar to that usually confronting healers: There is something terribly wrong. Things are not the way they should be. But the problem, in this view, is with the world, even though it may be manifest in the patient. Truth—and liberation theology, in contrast to much postmodern attitudinizing, believes in historical accuracy—is to be found in the perspective of those who suffer unjust privation.[30] Cornel West argues that "the condition of truth is to allow the suffering to speak. It doesn't mean that those who suffer have a monopoly on truth, but it means that the condition of truth to emerge must be in tune with those who are undergoing social misery—socially induced forms of suffering."[31]

The second lesson is that medicine has much to learn by reflecting on the lives and struggles of poor or otherwise oppressed people. How is suffering, including that caused by sickness, best explained? How is it to be addressed? These questions are, of course, as old as humankind. We've had millennia in which to address—societally, in an organized fashion—the suffering that surrounds us. In looking at approaches to such problems, one can easily discern three main trends: *charity, development,* and *social justice.*

Each of these might have much to recommend it, but it is my belief that the first two approaches are deeply flawed. Those who believe that charity is the answer to the world's problems often have a tendency—sometimes striking, sometimes subtle, and surely lurking in all of us—to regard those needing charity as intrinsically inferior. This is different from regarding the poor as powerless or impoverished because of historical processes and events (slavery, say, or unjust economic policies propped up by powerful parties). There is an enormous difference between seeing people as the victims of innate shortcomings and seeing them as the victims of structural violence. Indeed, it is likely that the struggle for rights is undermined whenever the history of unequal chances, and of oppression, is erased or distorted.

The approach of charity further presupposes that there will always be those who have and those who have not. This may or may not be true, but, again, there are costs to viewing the problem in this light. In *Pedagogy of the Oppressed*, Paulo Freire writes: "In order to have the continued opportunity to express their 'generosity,' the oppressors must perpetuate injustice as well. An unjust social order is the permanent fount of this 'generosity,' which is nourished by death, despair, and poverty." Freire's conclusion follows naturally enough: "True generosity consists precisely in fighting to destroy the causes which nourish false charity."[32] Given the twentieth century's marked tendency toward increasing economic inequity in the face of economic growth, the future holds plenty of false charity. All the recent chatter about "personal responsibility" from "compassionate conservatives" erases history in a manner embarrassingly expedient for themselves. In a study of food aid in the United States, Janet Poppendieck links a rise in "kindness" to a decline in justice:

> The resurgence of charity is at once a symptom and a cause of our society's failure to face up to and deal with the erosion of equality. It is a symptom in that it stems, in part at least, from an abandonment of our hopes for the elimination of poverty; it signifies a retreat from the goals as well as the means that characterized the Great Society. It is symptomatic of a pervasive despair about actually solving problems that has turned us toward ways of man-

aging them: damage control, rather than prevention. More significantly, and more controversially, the proliferation of charity *contributes* to our society's failure; to grapple in meaningful ways with poverty.[33]

It is possible, however, to overstate the case against charity—it is, after all, one of the four cardinal virtues, in many traditions. Sometimes holier-than-thou progressives dismiss charity when it is precisely the virtue demanded. In medicine, charity underpins the often laudable goal of addressing the needs of "underserved populations." To the extent that medicine responds to, rather than creates, underserved populations, charity will always have its place in medicine.

Unfortunately, a preferential option for the poor is all too often absent from charity medicine. First, charity medicine should avoid, at all costs, the temptation to ignore or hide the causes of excess suffering among the poor. Meredeth Turshen gives a jarring example from apartheid South Africa:

South African pediatricians may have developed an expertise in the understanding and treatment of malnutrition and its complications, but medical expertise does not change the system that gives rise to malnutrition nor the environment to which treated children return, an environment in which half of the children die before their fifth birthday. Malnutrition, in this context, is a direct result of the government's policies, which perpetuate the apartheid system and promote the poor health conditions and human rights violations.[34]

Second, charity medicine too frequently consists of secondhand, castoff services—leftover medicine—doled out in piecemeal fashion. How can we tell the difference between the proper place of charity in medicine and the doling out of leftovers? Many of us have been involved in these sorts of good works and have often heard a motto such as this: "The homeless poor are every bit as deserving of good medical care as the rest of us." The notion of a preferential option for the poor challenges us by reframing the motto: the homeless poor are *more* deserving of good medical care than the rest of us.[35] Whenever medicine seeks to reserve its finest services for the destitute sick, you can be sure that it is option-for-the-poor medicine.

What about development approaches?[36] Often, this perspective seems to regard progress and development as almost natural processes. The technocrats who design development projects—including a certain Péligre Dam, which three decades ago displaced the population we seek to serve in central Haiti—plead for patience. In due time, the technocrats tell the poor, if they speak to them at all, you too will share our standard of living. (After a generation, the reassurance may be changed to "if not you, your children.") And certainly, looking around us, we see everywhere the tangible benefits of scientific development. So who but a Luddite would object to development as touted by the technocrats?

According to liberation theology, progress for the poor is not likely to ensue from development approaches, which are based on a "liberal" view of poverty. Liberal views place the problem with the poor themselves: these people are backward and reject the technological fruits of modernity. With assistance from others, they too will, after a while, reach a higher level of development. Thus does the victim-blaming noted in the earlier discussion of tuberculosis recur in discussions of underdevelopment.

For many liberation theologians, developmentalism or reformism cannot be rehabilitated. George Pixley and Clodovis Boff use these terms to describe what they consider an "erroneous" view of poverty (in contrast to the "dialectical" explanation) in which the growth of poverty is dependent on the growth of wealth. Poverty today, they note, "is mainly the result of a contradictory development, in which the rich become steadily richer, and the poor become steadily poorer." Such a poverty is "internal to the system and a natural product of it."[37] Developmentalism not only erases the historical creation of poverty but also implies that development is necessarily a linear process: progress will inevitably occur if the right steps are followed. Yet any critical assessment of the impact of such approaches must acknowledge their failure to help the poor, as Leonardo and Clodovis Boff argue:

> "Reformism" seeks to improve the situation of the poor, but always within existing social relationships and the basic structuring of society, which rules out greater participation by all and diminution in the privileges enjoyed by the ruling classes. Reformism can lead to great feats of development in the poorer nations, but this development is nearly always at the expense of the oppressed poor and very rarely in their favor. For example, in 1964 the Brazilian economy ranked 46th in the world; in 1984 it ranked 8th. The last twenty years have seen undeniable technological and industrial progress, but at the same time there has been a considerable worsening of social conditions for the poor, with exploitation, destitution, and hunger on a scale previously unknown in Brazilian history. This has been the price paid by the poor for this type of elitist, exploitative, and exclusivist development.[38]

In his Introduction to *A Theology of Liberation*, Gustavo Gutiérrez concurs: we assert our humanity, he argues, in "the struggle to construct a just and fraternal society, where persons can live with dignity and be the agents of their own destiny. It is my opinion that the term *development* does not well express these profound aspirations."[39] Gutiérrez continues by noting that the term "liberation" expresses the hopes of the poor much more succinctly. Phillip Berryman puts it even more sharply: "'Liberation' entails a break with the present order in which Latin American countries could establish sufficient autonomy to reshape their economies to serve the needs of that poor majority. The term 'liberation' is understood in contradistinction to 'development.'"[40]

In examining medicine, one sees the impact of "developmental" thinking not only in the planned obsolescence of medical technology, essential to the process of commodification, but also in influential analytic constructs such as the "health transition model."[41] In this view, societies as they develop are making their way toward that great transition, when deaths will no longer be caused by infections such as tuberculosis but will occur much later and be caused by heart disease and cancer. But this model masks interclass differences *within* a particular country. For the poor, wherever they live, there is, often enough, no health transition. In other words, wealthy citizens of "underdeveloped" nations (those countries that have not yet experienced their health transition) do not die young from infectious diseases; they die later and from the same diseases that claim similar populations in wealthy countries. In parts of Harlem, in contrast, death rates in certain age groups are as high as those in Bangladesh; in both places, the leading causes of death in young adults are infections and violence.[42]

The powerful, including heads of state and influential policymakers, are of course impatient with such observations and respond, if they deign to respond, with sharp reminders that the overall trends are the results that count. But if we focus exclusively on aggregate data, why not declare public health in Latin America a resounding success? After all, life expectancies have climbed; infant and maternal mortality have dropped. But if you work in the service of the poor, what's happening to that particular class, whether in Harlem or in Haiti, always counts a great deal. In fact, it counts most. And from this vantage point—the one demanded by liberation theology—neither medicine nor development looks nearly so successful. In fact, the outcome gap between rich and poor has continued to grow.

In summary, then, the charity and development models, though perhaps useful at times, are found wanting in rigorous and soul-searching examination. That leaves the social justice model. In my experience, people who work for social justice, regardless of their own station in life, tend to see the world as deeply flawed. They see the conditions of the poor not only as unacceptable but as the result of structural violence that is human-made. As Robert McAfee Brown, paraphrasing the Uruguayan Jesuit Juan Luis Segundo, observes, "Unless we agree that the world should not be the way it is . . . there is no point of contact, because the world that is satisfying to us is the same world that is utterly devastating to them."[43] Often, if these individuals are privileged people like me, they understand that they have been implicated, whether directly or indirectly, in the creation or maintenance of this structural violence. They then feel indignation, but also humility and penitence. Where I work, this is easy: I see the Péligre Dam almost every week.

This posture—of penitence and indignation—is critical to effective social justice work. Alas, it is all too often absent or, worse, transformed from posture into posturing. And unless the posture is linked to much more pragmatic interventions, it usually fizzles out.

Fortunately, embracing these concepts and this posture do have very concrete implications. Making an option for the poor inevitably implies working for social justice, working with poor people as they struggle to change their situations. In a world riven by inequity, medicine could be viewed as social justice work. In fact, doctors are far more fortunate than most modern professionals: we still have a sliver of hope for meaningful, dignified service to the oppressed. Few other disciplines can make this claim with any honesty. We have a lot to offer right now. In Haiti and Peru and Chiapas, we have found that it is often less a question of "development" and more one of redistribution of goods and services, of simply sharing the fruits of science and technology. The majority of our efforts in the transfer of technology—medications, laboratory supplies, computers, and training—are conceived in just this way. They end up being innovative for other reasons: it is almost unheard of to insist that the destitute sick receive high-quality care as a right.

Treating poor Peruvians who suffer from multidrug-resistant tuberculosis according to the highest standard of care, rather than according to whatever happens to be deemed "cost-effective," is not only social justice work but also, ironically enough, innovative. Introducing antiretroviral medications, and the health systems necessary to use them wisely, to AIDS-afflicted rural Haiti is, again, viewed as pie-in-the-sky by international health specialists but as only fitting by liberation theology. For example, operating rooms (and cesarean sections) must be part of any "minimum package" of health services wherever the majority of maternal deaths are caused by cephalopelvic disproportion. This is obvious from the perspective of social justice but controversial in international health circles. And the list goes on.

A preferential option for the poor also implies a mode of analyzing health systems. In examining tuberculosis in Haiti, for example, our analysis must be *historically deep*—not merely deep enough to recall an event such as that which deprived most of my patients of their land, but deep enough to remember that modern-day Haitians are the descendants of a people enslaved in order to provide our ancestors with cheap sugar, coffee, and cotton.

Our analysis must be *geographically broad*. In this increasingly interconnected world ("the world that is satisfying to us is the same world that is utterly devastating to them"), we must understand that what happens to poor people is never divorced from the actions of the powerful. Certainly, people who define themselves as poor may control their own destinies to some extent. But control of lives is related to control of land, systems of production, and the formal political and legal structures in which lives are enmeshed. With time, both wealth and control have become increasingly concentrated in the hands of a few. The opposite trend is desired by those working for social justice.

For those who work in Latin America, the role of the United States looms large. Father James Guadalupe Carney, a Jesuit priest, put his life on the line in order to serve the poor of Honduras. As far as we can tell, he was killed by US-trained Honduran security forces in 1983.[44] In an introduction to his posthumously published autobiography, his sister and brother-in-law asked starkly: "Do we North Americans eat well because the poor in the third world do not eat at all? Are we North Americans powerful, because we help keep the poor in the third world weak? Are we North Americans free, because we help keep the poor in the third world oppressed?"[45]

Granted, it is difficult enough to "think globally and act locally." But perhaps what we are really called to do, in efforts to make common cause with the poor, is to think locally and globally and to act in response to both levels of analysis. If we fail in this task, we may never be able to contend with the structures that create and maintain poverty, structures that make people sick. Although physicians and nurses, even those who serve the poor, have not followed liberation theology, its insights have never been more relevant to our vocation. As international health experts come under the sway of the bankers and their curiously bounded utilitarianism, we can expect more and more of our services to be declared "cost-ineffective" and more of our patients to be erased. In declaring health and health care to be a human right, we join forces with those who have long labored to protect the rights and dignity of the poor.

Notes

[1] Boff 1989, 23.

[2] The literature on the correlation between poverty, inequality, and increased morbidity and mortality is massive. For reviews, see, for example, Farmer 1999; Kim, Millen, Irwin, and Gershman 2000; and Wilkinson 1996. Other major reviews include Leclerc, Fassin, Grandjean, et al. 2000; World Health Organization 1999, 2000; World Bank 2000; Bartley, Blane, and Smith 1998; Sen 1998; Coburn 2000; and Fiscella, Franks, Gold, et al. 2000. Other articles review case studies of inequality in access to treatment of specific diseases; see, for example, Rathore, Berger, Weinfurt, et al. 2000; and of course the sizable body of literature on inequality of access to HIV therapy.

[3] Gutiérrez 1983, 44.

[4] For a concise history of liberation theology, its historical relevance, and an

explanation of key themes and motivations, see Leonardo and Clodovis Boff's slim and helpful volume *Introducing Liberation Theology* (1987).

⁵ Base-community movements, also known as "basic ecclesial communities," are disparate and sociologically complex, and I do not aspire to review their idealized or actual impact. But, as this movement has been felt throughout Latin America, I would encourage further reading. For an insider account, see the volume by Father Alvaro Barreiro (1982). A study by John Burdick (1993) contains a complementary, scholarly examination of such communities in urban Brazil.

⁶ There are other clues that liberation theology might have something to offer the healing professions: for one, the more destructive forces hate it. In 1982, for example, advisers to US President Ronald Reagan argued that "American foreign policy must begin to counterattack (and not just react against) liberation theology" (quoted from the Santa Fe Document, a Reagan administration working paper); cited in Boff and Boff 1987, p. 86).

⁷ Health care "reforms" in Latin America and other developing regions starting in the last part of the twentieth century have followed a neoliberal framework that favors commercialization, corporatization, and privatization of health and social welfare services. Most notable is the enthusiastic exportation of the US model of "managed care." As Neill notes in his critique of these developments, "managed health care is touted by many experts—usually found in USAID, the World Bank, and various havens of academia—as a tangible model which can be of immense value to developing countries if applied wisely and efficiently" (2001, 61). This position, of course, ignores the growing body of evidence challenging the unabashed claims that managed-care organizations (MCOs) provide quality care with efficiency and cost-effectiveness—evidence that also points to managed care's role in exacerbating the already large inequities that characterize health care in the United States (Anders 1996; Andrulis and Carrier 1999; Farmer and Rylko-Bauer 2001; Ginzberg 1999; Himmelstein, Woolhandler, and Hellander 2001; Lewin and Altman 2000; Maskovsky 2000; Pellegrino 1999; Peterson 1999; Schneider, Zaslavsky, and Epstein 2002).

In fact, Waitzkin and Iriart note that, as the US market has become saturated and MCOs face growing criticism, these corporations

> have turned their eyes toward developing countries, especially those in Latin America. In the tradition of tobacco and pesticides, U.S. corporations are exporting to developing countries—in the form of managed care—products and practices that have come under heavy criticism domestically. The exportation of managed care is also receiving enthusiastic support from the World Bank, other multilateral lending agencies, and multinational corporations. . . . Developing countries are experiencing strong pressure to accept managed care as the organizational framework for privatization of their health and social security systems. . . . This ex-

perience is serving as a model for the exportation of managed care to Africa and Asia. (2001, 497)

There is, of course, much money to be made by tapping into the health care and social security funds of the public sector even in poorer developing nations, under the guise of rescuing these countries from inefficient bureaucracies and rising costs by importing neoliberal managed-care solutions. Large segments of the population in Latin America live in poverty and often have minimal or no access to formal health care. The consequences of such health care transformations for the poor and the oppressed in developing countries, as well as for the public health systems they might rely on, are dire, to say the least. "As public health systems are dismantled and privatized under the auspices of managed care, multi-national corporations predictably will enter the field, reap vast profits, and exit within several years. Then developing countries will face the awesome prospect of reconstructing their public systems" (Waitzkin and Iriart 2001, 498). For more on health care reforms in Latin America, see Armada, Muntaner, and Navarro 2001; Barraza-Lloréns, Bertozzi, González-Pier, et al. 2002; Iriart, Merhy, and Waitzkin 2001; Laurell 2001; Pérez-Stable 1999; and Stocker, Waitzkin, and Iriart 1999.

[8] Segundo 1980, 16; quoted from Segunda Conferencia General del Episcopado Latinoamericano, Medellín 1968.

[9] Boff 1989, 20.

[10] Eagleson and Scharper 1979, 128.

[11] Gutiérrez 1983, 87.

[12] Sobrino explains the link between structural violence and structural sin: "God's creation is being assaulted and vitiated. . . . because this reality is not simply natural, but historical—being the result of action taken by some human beings against others—this reality is sinful. As absolute negation of God's will, this sinfulness is very serious and fundamental" (1988, 15).

[13] Pixley and Boff 1989, 242.

[14] In the English translation of *Pedagogy of the Oppressed,* the original Portuguese term is retained. In Freire's own words, *"Conscientização* is the deepening of the attitude of awareness characteristic of all emergence"—in other words, critical consciousness (1986, 101).

[15] Brown 1993, 45.

[16] Sobrino 1988, 31.

[17] Ibid., 13, 15.

[18] Brown 1993, 45.

[19] Sobrino 1988, 31.

[20] "Communiqué from the CCRI-CG of the EZLN, January 6, 1994," in Marcos and the Zapatista Army of National Liberation 1995, 58.

[21] See Farmer 1999, chap. 1; and Farmer and Nardell 1998.

[22] Even at the dawn of the era of antibiotics, when streptomycin was already available, class divisions were sharp inside Europe's sanatoriums. George Orwell's journal entries from the year before his death of tuberculosis are telling:

> Curious effect, here in the sanitorium, on Easter Sunday, when the people in this (the most expensive) block of "chalets" mostly have visitors, of hearing large numbers of upper-class English voices. I have been almost out to the sound of them for two years, hearing them at most one or two at a time, my ears growing more and more used to working-class or lower-middle-class Scottish voices. In the hospital at Hairmyres, for instance, I literally never heard a "cultivated" accent except when I had a visitor. It is as though I were hearing these voices for the first time. And what voices! A sort of over-fedness, a fatuous self-confidence, a constant bah-bahing of laughter about nothing, above all a sort of heaviness and richness combined with a fundamental ill-will—people who, one instinctively feels, without even being able to see them, are the enemies of anything intelligent or sensitive or beautiful. No wonder everyone hates us so. (Journal entry from April 17, 1949; Orwell 1968, 578).

For more on the history of tuberculosis in North America, see Georgina Feldberg's (1995) helpful review; see also the classic study by Dubos and Dubos (1952.). Unfortunately, little has been written of the history of tuberculosis in the regions of the world where it has taken its greatest toll.

[23] For an overview of the burden of disease and death caused by *M. tuberculosis,* see Farmer, Walton, and Becerra 2000.

[24] These "twists" are reviewed in Farmer 1999, chap. 9.

[25] This story is told more fully in Farmer 1992, 19–27.

[26] For a more detailed discussion of this study, see Farmer 1999, 217–25.

[27] Farmer 1990.

[28] Farmer, Robin, Ramilus, et al. 1991, 260. For more on this project, see Farmer 1999, chap. 8.

[29] Indeed, one does not need to ascribe directly to the religious tenets of liberation theology in order to make a "preferential option for the poor." Pixley and Boff summarize the widespread starvation, malnutrition, and poverty that are a daily reality for millions (remarking that one does not need "socio-scientific instruments" to prove this) and conclude that "this state of affairs is *morally intolerable,* for those who do not believe in the God of the Bible as much as for those who do" (1989, 238, 239). They note the simple facts of the situation and what our response—whether one imbued with faith, or one relying solely on reason—must logically be:

The energy to find the solution can come only from the oppressed themselves. Wherever there is oppression, there will be struggles to win life-sustaining conditions—struggles between classes, between races, between nations, between sexes. This is simply an observable fact, not a moral imperative or a scientific conclusion. We can see the just struggles of the oppressed going on around us, and we cannot see any other way out of the vast problems that afflict humanity at the close of the twentieth century. (242)

For a more in-depth discussion of these matters, refer to the full argument made by Pixley and Boff (1989, 237–43).

[30] Perhaps it goes without saying that no physician who bases his or her practice on clinical trials can in good faith buy into the postmodern argument that all claims to truth are merely "competing discourses." But, as Christopher Norris writes, in both the social sciences and the humanities, the conviction that we ought to find out what really happened is proof

> that we hadn't caught up with the "postmodern" rules of the game, the fact that nowadays things have moved on to the point where there is no last ground of appeal to those old, self-deluding "enlightenment" values that once possessed authority (or the semblance thereof), at least in some quarters. Anyone who continues to invoke such standards is plainly in the grip of a nostalgic desire for some ultimate truth-telling discourse—whether Platonist, Kantian, Marxist, or whatever—that would offers delusionary refuge from the knowledge that we are nowadays utterly without resources in the matter of distinguishing truth from falsehood. (1992, 13)

Norris's devastating account of intellectuals and the Gulf War (1992) is one of the best critiques of the postmodern foolishness that has gained quite a foothold in universities on both sides of the Atlantic. See also Norris 1990.

[31] West 1993, 4.

[32] Freire 1986, 29.

[33] Poppendieck 1998, 5.

[34] Turshen 1986, 891.

[35] Samuel Johnson once observed that "a decent provision for the poor is the true test of civilization." Surely this is true, and it serves as an indictment of affluent society. But liberation theology delivers an even more damning indictment, since its proponents argue that we should reserve our highest standards for the poor.

[36] My critique of development is by no means original; it draws heavily on

a very large literature reaching back almost thirty years. From Andre Gunder Frank to Immanuel Wallerstein, the more refined versions of dependency theory cannot be lightly dismissed. For more recent reviews of the limitations of development approaches to health care, see Meredeth Turshen's wonderful book *Privatizing Health Services in Africa* (1999).

[37] Pixley and Boff 1989, 6–7.

[38] Boff and Boff 1987, 5.

[39] Gutiérrez 1973, xiv.

[40] Berryman 1987, 91.

[41] For an introduction to the notion of health transition, see Caldwell, Findley, Caldwell, et al. 1990; Zielinski-Gutiérrez and Kendall (2000) have more recently qualified this concept by placing it in a broader social context. See also the discussion by Mosley, Bobadilla, and Jamison (1993) on the implications of this model for developing countries.

[42] McCord and Freeman 1990.

[43] Brown 1993, 44.

[44] Carney is said to have been killed after being captured when he participated in an ill-fated guerrilla incursion from Nicaragua into Olancho Province, Honduras.

[45] Carney 1987, xi. Carney goes on to criticize the United States directly, citing the US-backed 1973 military coup d'etat in Chile, in which tens of thousands were killed, as his own moment of realization about the extent of the often brutal US involvement in the political and economic affairs of the region: "After the bloody military coup of 1973 in Chile, *it was obvious that the United States would never allow a country that is economically dependent on it to make a revolution by means of elections*—through the democratic process directed by the majority—at least as long as the country has an army that obeys the capitalist bourgeoisie of the country" (311). For an examination of US policy toward progressive movements in Guatemala, El Salvador, and Haiti in a similar light, see Farmer 1994.

References

Anders, G. 1996. *Health against Wealth: HMOs and the Breakdown of Medical Trust.* Boston: Houghton Mifflin.

Andrulis, D. P., and B. Carrier. 1999. *Managed Care in the Inner City: The Uncertain Promise for Providers, Plans, and Communities.* San Francisco: Jossey-Bass.

Armada, F., C. Muntaner, and V. Navarro. 2001. "Health and Social Security Reforms in Latin America: The Convergence of the World Health Organization, the World Bank, and Transnational Corporations." *International Journal of Health Services* 31 (4): 729–68.

Barraza-Lloréns, M., S. Bertozzi, E. González-Pier, et al. 2002. "Addressing Inequality in Health and Health Care in Mexico." *Health Affairs* 21 (3): 47–56.

Barreiro, A. 1982. *Basic Ecclesial Communities: The Evangelization of the Poor.* Maryknoll, NY: Orbis Books.

Bartley, M., D. Blane, and G. D. Smith. 1998. "Introduction: Beyond the Black Report." *Sociology of Health and Illness* 20 (5): 563–77.

Berryman, P. 1987. *Liberation Theology: Essential Facts about the Revolutionary Movement in Latin America and Beyond.* New York: Pantheon.

Boff, L. 1989. *Faith on the Edge: Religion and Marginalized Existence.* San Francisco: Harper and Row.

Boff, L., and C. Boff. 1987. *Introducing Liberation Theory.* Mary-knoll, NY: Orbis Books.

Brown, R. M. 1993. *Liberation Theology: An Introductory Guide.* Louisville: Westminster/John Knox.

Burdick, J. 1993. *Looking for God in Brazil: The Progressive Catholic Church in Urban Brazil's Religious Arena.* Berkeley: University of California Press.

Caldwell, J. C., S. Findley, P. Caldwell, et al., eds. 1990. *What We Know about Health Transition: The Cultural, Social, and Behavioural Determinants of Health. The Proceedings of an International Workshop, Canberra, May 1989.* Canberra: Health Transition Centre, Australian National University.

Carney, J. G. 1987. *To Be a Revolutionary.* San Francisco: Harper and Row.

Coburn, D. 2000. "Income Inequality, Social Cohesion, and the Health Status of Populations: The Role of Neo-Liberalism." *Social Science and Medicine* 51 (1): 135–46.

Dubos, R., and J. Dubos. 1952. *The White Plague: Tuberculosis, Man, and Society.* Boston: Little, Brown.

Eagleson, J., and P. Scharper, eds. 1979. *Puebla and Beyond: Documentation and Commentary.* Maryknoll, NY: Orbis Books.

Farmer, P. E. 1990. "Sending Sickness: Sorcery, Politics, and Changing Concepts of AIDS in Rural Haiti." *Medical Anthropology Quarterly* 4 (1): 6–27.

———. 1992. *AIDS and Accusation: Haiti and the Geography of Blame.* Berkeley: University of California Press.

———. 1994. *The Uses of Haiti.* Monroe, ME: Common Courage Press.

———. 1999. *Infections and Inequalities: The Modern Plagues.* Berkeley: University of California Press.

Farmer, P. E., and E. Nardell. 1998. "Nihilism and Pragmatism in Tuberculosis Control." *American Journal of Public Health* 88 (7): 1014–15.

Farmer, P. E., S. Robin, and S. L. Ramilus, et al. 1991. "Tuberculosis, Poverty, and 'Compliance': Lessons from Rural Haiti." *Seminars in Respiratory Infections* 6 (4): 254–60.

Farmer, P. E., and B. Rylko-Bauer. 2001. "L' 'exceptionnel' systéme de santé américain: Critique d'une médecine à vocation commerciale" (The "exceptional" American health care system: Critique of the for-profit approach). *Actes de la Recherche en Sciences Sociales* 139:13–30.

Farmer, P. E., D. A. Walton, and M. C. Becerra. 2000. "International Tuberculosis Control in the 21st Century." In *Tuberculosis: Current Concepts and Treatment,* 2nd ed., ed. L. N. Friedman, 475–96. Boca Raton: CRC Press.

Feldberg, G. 1995. *Disease and Class: Tuberculosis and the Shaping of Modern North American Society.* New Brunswick, NJ: Rutgers University Press.

Fiscella, K., P. Franks, M. R. Gold, et al. 2000. "Inequality in Quality: Addressing Socioeconomic, Racial, and Ethnic Disparities in Health Care." *JAMA* 283 (19): 2579–84.

Freire, P. *The Pedagogy of the Oppressed.* New York: Continuum.

Ginzberg, E. 1999. "The Uncertain Future of Managed Care." *New England Journal of Medicine* 340 (2): 144–46.

Gutiérrez, G. 1973. *A Theology of Liberation: History, Politics, and Salvation.* Maryknoll, NY: Orbis Books.

———. 1983. *The Power of the Poor in History.* Maryknoll, NY: Orbis Books.

Himmelstein, D., S. Woolhandler, and I. Hellander. 2001. *Bleeding the Patient: The Consequences of Corporate Health Care.* Monroe, ME: Common Courage Press.

Iriart, C., E. E. Merhy, and H. Waitzkin. 2001. "Managed Care in Latin America: The New Common Sense in Health Policy Reform." *Social Science and Medicine* 52 (8): 1243–53.

Kim, J. Y., J. V. Millen, A. Irwin, and J. Gershman, eds. 2000. *Dying for Growth: Global Inequality and the Health of the Poor.* Monroe, ME: Common Courage Press.

Laurell, A. C. 2001. "Health Reform in Mexico: The Promotion of Inequality." *International Journal of Health Services* 31 (2): 291–321.

Leclerc, A. D. Fassin, H. Grandjean, et al., eds. 2000. *Les inégalités sociales de santé.* Paris: Éditions la Découverte et Syros.

Lewin, M. E., and S. Altman, eds. 2000. *America's Health Care Safety Net: Intact but Endangered.* Washington, DC: National Academy Press.

Marcos, S., and the Zapatista Army of National Liberation. 1995. *Shadows of Tender Fury: The Letters and Communiqués of Subcomandante Marcos and the Zapatista Army of National Liberation.* New York: Monthly Review Press.

Maskovsky, J. 2000. "'Managing' the Poor: Neoliberalism, Medicaid HMOs, and the Triumph of Consumerism among the Poor." *Medical Anthropology* 19 (2): 121–46.

McCord, C., and H. Freeman. 1990. "Excess Mortality in Harlem." *New England Journal of Medicine* 322 (3): 173–77.

Mosley, W. H., J. L. Bobadilla, and D. T. Jamison. 1993. "The Health Transition: Implications for Health Policy in Developing Countries." In *Disease Control Priorities in Developing Countries,* ed. D. T. Jamison, W. H. Mosley, A. R. Measham, and J. L. Bobadilla, 673–99. New York: Oxofrd Medical Publications.

Neill, K. G. 2001. "Dancing with the Devil: Health, Human Rights, and the Export of US Models of Managed Care to Developing Countries." *Cultural Survival Quarterly* 24 (4): 61–63.

Norris, C. 1990. *What's Wrong with Postmodernism: Critical Theory and the Ends of Philosophy.* Baltimore: Johns Hopkins University Press.

———. 1992. *Uncritical Theory: Postmodernism, Intellectuals, and the Gulf War.* Amherst: University of Massachusetts Press.

Orwell, G. 1968. *The Collected Essays, Journalism, and Letters of George Orwell.* Vol. 4: *In Front of Your Nose, 1945–1950.* New York: Penguin Books.

Pellegrino, E. 1999. "The Commodification of Medical and Health Care: The Moral Consequences of a Paradigm Shift from a Professional to a Market Ethic." *Journal of Medicine and Philosophy* 24 (3): 243–66.

Pérez-Stable, E. J. 1999. "Managed Care Arrives in Latin America." *New England Journal of Medicine* 340 (14): 1110–12.

Peterson, M. A., ed. 1999. "Managed Care Backlash." Special issue. *Journal of Health Politics, Policy, and Law* 24 (5): 873–1218.

Pixley, G. V., and C. Boff. 1989. *The Bible, the Church, and the Poor.* Maryknoll, NY: Orbis Books.

Poppendieck, J. 1998. *Sweet Charity? Emergency Food and the End of Entitlements.* New York: Viking Press.

Rathore, S. S., A. K. Berger, K. P. Weinfurt, et al. 2000. "Race, Sex, Poverty, and the Medical Treatment of Acute Myocardial Infarction in the Elderly." *Circulation: Journal of the American Heart Association* 102 (6): 642–48.

Schneider, E. C., A. M. Zaslavsky, and A. M. Epstein. 2002. "Racial Disparities in the Qualtiy of Care for Enrollees in Medicare Managed Care." *JAMA* 287 (10): 1288–94.

Segundo, J. L. 1976. *Our Idea of God.* Dublin: Gill and Macmillan.

Sen, A. 1998. "Mortality as an Indicator of Economic Success and Failure." *Economic Journal* 108 (446): 1–25.

Sobrino, J. 1988. *Spirituality of Liberation: Toward Political Holiness.* Maryknoll, NY: Orbis Books.

Stocker, K., H. Waitzkin, and C. Iriart. 1999. "The Exportation of Managed Care to Latin America." *New England Journal of Medicine* 340 (14): 1131–36.

Turshen, M. 1986. "Health and Human Rights in a South African Bantustan." *Social Science and Medicine* 22 (9): 887–92.

———. 1999. *Privatizing Health Services in Africa.* New Brunswick, NJ: Rutgers University Press.

Waitzkin, H., and C. Iriart. 2000. "How the United States Exports Managed Care to Third World Countries." *Monthly Review* 52 (1): 21–35.

West, C. 1993. *Prophetic Thought in Postmodern Times.* Monroe, ME: Common Courage Press.

Wilkinson, R. G. 1996. *Unhealthy Societies: The Afflictions of Inequality.* London: Routledge.

World Bank. 2000. *The Burden of Disease among the Global Poor: Current Situation, Future Trends, and Implications for Strategy.* Washington, DC: World Bank.

World Health Organization. 1999. *World Health Report 1999—Making a Difference.* Geneva: World Health Organization.

———. 2000. *World Health Report 2000: Health Systems: Improving Performance.* Geneva: World Health Organization.

Zielinski Gutiérrez, E. C., and C. Kendall. 2000. "The Globalization of Health and Disease: The Health Transition and Global Change." In *The Handbook of Social Studies in Health and Medicine,* ed. G. Albrecht, R. Fitzpatrick, and S. Scrimshaw, 84–99. London: Sage.

4

Conversion

A Requirement for Solidarity

Gustavo Gutiérrez

A conversion is the starting point of every spiritual journey.[1] It involves a break with the life lived up to that point; it is a prerequisite for entering the kingdom: "The time is fulfilled, and the kingdom of God is at hand; repent, and believe in the gospel" (Mk 1:15). It presupposes also, and above all, that one decides to set out on a new path: "Sell all that you have . . . and come, follow me" (Lk 18:22).[2] Without this second aspect the break would lack the focus that a fixed horizon provides and would ultimately be deprived of meaning.

Because of this second aspect a conversion is not something that is done once and for all. It entails a development, even a painful one, that is not without uncertainties, doubts, and temptations to turn back on the road that has been traveled. The experience of the Jewish people after departure from Egypt is still prototypical here. Fidelity to the word of God implies a permanent conversion. This is a central theme in the teaching of the prophets.

On the other hand, the path of conversion is not one marked only by stumbling blocks; there is a growth in maturity. Throughout the gospels we are repeatedly told that after some

---

This chapter contains chapter 6 and part of chapter 7 from *We Drink from Our Own Wells: The Spiritual Journey of a People* (1984; Maryknoll, NY: Orbis Books, 2003), 95–113.

word or deed of Jesus "his disciples believed in him." The point of this statement is not that up to that point they had no faith, but rather that their faith deepened with the passage of time. To believe in God is more than simply to profess God's existence; it is to enter into communion with God and—the two being inseparable—with our fellow human beings as well. And all this adds up to a process.

Break and Solidarity

Break, new way, steps forward and backward—this entire movement is subject to the call and action of the Spirit who requires of us a decision that leads us to think, feel, and live with Christ in our day-to-day lives (Phil 2:5). This requirement is seen as especially urgent by Christians committed, in one way or another, to the liberation of the poor in Latin America.

The upshot of the option for the poor and their liberation is that in contemporary Latin America we are in a period characterized by a great effort at solidarity. Solidarity is seen as a concrete expression of Christian love today, which seeks roots in the cultural traditions of the indigenous peoples of Latin America. A hasty and simplistic interpretation of the liberationist perspective has led some to affirm that its dominant, if not exclusive, themes are commitment, the social dimension of faith, the denunciation of injustices, and others of a similar nature. It is said that the liberationist impulse leaves little room for grasping the necessity of personal conversion as a condition for Christian life and for being aware of the place that sin and repentance have in our lives.

Such an interpretation and criticism are simply caricatures. One need only have contact with the Christians in question to appreciate the complexity of their approach and the depth of their spiritual experience. In the movement of solidarity with the poor and exploited there is no attempt to downplay the importance of the breaks that the gospel demands of us as a requirement for accepting the message of the kingdom; if anything, the movement calls rather for an emphasis on this factor. The period of solidarity that men and women are experiencing in Latin America is leading to a new grasp of the importance of conversion; in doing so it gives us insight into aspects of which no account is taken in other approaches, and it is perhaps this that is confusing some observers.

Acknowledgment of Sin

In our relationship with God and with others there is an inescapable personal dimension: to reject a fellow human—a possibility implicit in our freedom—is to reject God as well. Conversion implies that we recognize the presence of sin in our lives and our world. In other words, we see and admit what is vitiating our relationship with God and our solidarity with others—what, in consequence, is also hindering the creation of a just and human society. The situation of tragic poverty in which Latin America is living only intensifies this awareness on our part.

To sin is to deny love, to resist welcoming the Kingdom of God. Many of those who are committed to the poor freely admit the difficulties they have, as human beings and believers, in loving God and neighbor and therefore their need of repentance and a break with deviant practices. A Christian community in Lima writes: "There are defects in our lives. Sin is among us too, and we are not always faithful. We do not always live up to our commitments; there are little betrayals, acts of cowardice, falls, selfish and underhanded actions." Unless we see our personal connivances with elements that are keeping an inhuman and unjust situation in existence, we run the risk of pharisaism: of seeing the speck in our neighbor's eye but not the beam in our own.

One type of connivance, which is clearer today now that we have a better knowledge of our social reality, takes the form of sins of omission: "We regard ourselves as guilty for keeping silence in the face of the events agitating our country. In the face of repression, detentions, the economic crisis, the loss of jobs by so many workers, murders and tortures, we have kept silent as though we did not belong to that world."[3] The cowardice that keeps silent in the face of the sufferings of the poor and that offers any number of adroit justifications represents an especially serious failure of Latin American Christians. However, it is not always easy to be lucid in this regard.

In addition, the bishops at Medellín, after speaking of individual failures, went on to say: "When speaking of injustice, we refer to those realities that constitute a sinful situation" ("Peace," no. 1). Despite the reactions to this point in some circles, Puebla endorsed what Medellín had said[4] and followed closely the guidelines set down by John Paul II in his Mexican addresses that were delivered during the very days when the Episcopal Conference was being held.[5]

Insofar, then, as a conversion is a break with sin it will have to have both a personal and a social dimension. The Episcopal Conference of Peru has stated:

> The good news we proclaim is not simply a past event; it has to do with the needs and aspirations of the human beings who hear it. At the same time it is an energetic call to a conversion that, although affecting the deepest recesses of the human person, is not limited to interior life but must also be translated into attitudes and commitments that regard changes in reality as a requirement of Christian love.[6]

Cardinal Juan Landázuri, archbishop of Lima, repeated the same urgent call: "At the present time our native land is undergoing a painful crisis in which the high social cost paid in hunger and undernourishment, sickness, and death, lack of education and jobs . . . falls with special cruelty on the vast majority of our people. At such a time the call for personal conversion and social change becomes particularly urgent."[7]

The change called for is not simply an interior one but one that involves the entire person as a corporeal being (a factor of human solidarity) and therefore also has consequences for the web of social relationships of which the individual is a part. That is why Archbishop Romero could make this strong statement: "Nowadays an authentic Christian conversion must lead to an unmasking of the social mechanisms that turn the worker and the peasant into marginalized persons. Why do the rural poor become part of society only in the coffee- and cotton-picking seasons?"[8] The will to conversion should lead to this kind of concrete analysis.

For a long time this perspective has perhaps been absent from the treatment of the theme in spiritual literature; today, however, it cannot be neglected.[9] The encounter with the Lord in the inmost recesses of the individual does not exclude but rather calls for a similar encounter in the depths of the wretchedness in which the poor of our countries live. In these poor, Puebla tells us, "we ought to recognize the suffering features of Christ the Lord, who questions and challenges us." But how can we do this and achieve solidarity with the poor if we do not understand the structural causes of "this situation of pervasive extreme poverty" that gives rise to the suffering?

The consequences of such recognition are clear. It becomes necessary for us to examine our own responsibility for the existence of unjust "social mechanisms." In addition to calling for a personal transformation, the analysis will in many cases mean a break with the social milieu to which we belong. The conversion required will have to be radical enough to bring us into a different world, the world of the poor. I shall return to this point.

As in Saint Paul, sin means death. This is true both of personal sin and of the situation of sin in which Latin America is living. A commitment to the poor makes us see this truth with a new urgency, as Archbishop Romero put it:

> Now we realize what sin is. We realize that offenses against God bring death to human beings. We realize that sin is truly death-dealing; not only does it bring the interior

death of the one who commits it; it also produces real, objective death. We are thus reminded of a basic truth of our Christian faith. Sin caused the death of the Son of God; sin continues to cause the death of the children of God.[10]

This is a clear and profound statement that raises questions and points to new paths.

The Way of Life

To acknowledge one's sins implies the will to restore broken amity, to which we are called by petition for pardon and reconciliation. The God of the Bible manifests fidelity and mercy in a permanent disposition to pardon: "The steadfast love of the Lord never ceases, his mercies never come to an end" (Lam 3:22–23).

This attitude of God must serve as a model for the people of God. As Micah puts it, "He has showed you, O man, what is good; and what does the Lord require of you but to do justice, and to love kindness, and to walk humbly with your God?" (6:8). Pardon is an inherent characteristic of the Christian community. To pardon means not to fixate the past, but to create possibilities for persons to change and to realign the course of their lives. The Lord does not want us to have an "evil eye," trying to ossify persons and situations in movement; the Lord is good, merciful, and open to what is new (Mt 20:15). Pardon forges community.

The Bible tells us of a God who is faithful to and mindful of the divine deeds of the past, but also ready to forget, out of love, the failings of a sinful people. The psalmist can exclaim: "Thou didst withdraw all thy wrath; thou didst turn from thy hot anger" (85:3–4). Pardon implies forgetting, canceling out a past of death, and initiating a new era characterized by life. The psalmist would have us say confidently to the Lord: "Wilt thou not revive us again, that thy people may rejoice in thee?" (85:6).

The Lord is the one to whom we say, "Thou dost show me the path of life" (16:11). Exactly so!

The new way that conversion and pardon opens up takes the form of an option in behalf of life. The option finds expression particularly in solidarity with those who are subject to "a premature and unjust death." The bishop and priests of Machala, Ecuador, have stated:

> As the followers of Christ that we are trying to be, we cannot fail to show our solidarity with the suffering—the imprisoned, the marginalized, the persecuted—for Christ identifies himself with them (Mt 25:31–46). We once again assure the people of our support and our service in the fulfillment of our specific mission as preachers of the gospel of Jesus Christ who came to proclaim the good news to the poor and freedom to the oppressed. (Lk 4:18)[11]

This solidarity is not only with isolated individuals. To be poor is something much vaster and more complete than simply belonging to a specific social group (social class, culture, ethnos). By the same token, the context of a collectivity whose destiny is shared, willy-nilly, by the great majority of a given population must be taken into account. If, then, in our activity we try to separate them from their own world, we are not really in solidarity with them. If we love others, we love them in their social context. This requirement makes commitment more demanding but also more authentic.

For analogous reasons this way of solidarity is not to be undertaken by isolated individuals. It should be done along with the entire church. "We affirm," said the bishops at Puebla, "the need for conversion on the part of the whole church to a preferential option for the poor, an option aimed at their integral liberation" (Puebla Document, no. 1134; cf. 1157, 1158 [in *Puebla and Beyond,* ed. Eagleson and Scharper]). This conversion entails a break with a previous situation in which, for one or another reason, solidarity with the poor either did not exist or existed only as a possibility. This represents a deep-seated conviction among Latin

American Christians, and bishops laid a special emphasis on it even before Puebla. The Episcopal Conference of Guatemala has said: "The entire church of Guatemala must take part in the process of conversion in order that it may be an efficacious sign of Christ's presence in society and a suitable instrument in God's hands for contributing to the building of a better homeland."[12]

Conversion is a requirement for the solidarity that is part of the task of the church. Clergymen in Santiago, Chile, have stated:

> The bishops are conscious that one element in the mission of the church is to take up the work of solidarity, because in the final analysis solidarity is just another name for the ancient commandment the church has received from Jesus Christ. It used to be called mercy, then charity, then commitment; today it is called solidarity. To give food to the hungry . . . drink to the thirsty . . . clothing to the naked . . . shelter to the homeless . . . and to welcome the stranger are actions so basic that at the end of time we shall have to render an account of them. Solidarity is written into the very substance of the church, and therefore there can be no drawing back from the work needed to achieve it.[13]

In point of fact, the various terms mentioned are not perfectly interchangeable. They express different aspects of a single ecclesial function that the term "solidarity" serves to define very accurately in our day, for, as John Paul II has said, solidarity is a proof of the fidelity of the church to its Lord.[14]

The Material and the Spiritual

In the context of solidarity with the poor and oppressed, that which is often referred to as "the material" takes on a meaning it does not seem to have had before.

In recent decades an important revolution, and one ratified by Vatican II, has taken place in Christian experience and thought with regard to the value set on earthly realities.[15] This has led, among other results, to a new approach to the human body, despite reservations on the part of some. Encouraged by this new perspective, some Christian milieus, usually in affluent countries, have promoted a reevaluation and "celebration" of the human body in cultural expressions—for example, some modern dances and other bodily forms of expression that are used in eucharistic celebrations. In their desire to break with a spirituality that they think belittles or neglects the physical side of their lives, these Christians emphasize the importance of the bodily expressions of Christian life; more broadly, they stress the rights of the body (their own bodies) in human life.

Whatever be the merits of this claim, I want to note here that the concern for the corporeal in contemporary Latin American spiritual experiences has come about in quite a different way. There is no question here of a preoccupation with the physical and material dimensions of our individual selves. In our world, there has been a breakthrough of the material because the vast majorities are in urgent need of bread, medicine, housing, and so on. The physical in question is located at the level of the basic necessities of the human person. It is not "my body" but the "body of the poor person"—the weak and languishing body of the poor— that has made the material a part of a spiritual outlook.[16] The goal is to liberate that body from the forces of death, and this liberation entails a walking according to the Spirit who is life. In this, Paul is a guide without equal.

The religious aspirations of the poor do not eliminate their physical hunger, and we must keep both of these dimensions before us. As Rutilio Grande recalled, "It was correctly said during our Archdiocesan Pastoral Week that 'our people are hungry for the true God and they are hungry for bread.' And no privileged minority has any right, from the Christian standpoint, to exist in isolation in our country; it can exist only in function of the great majorities that make up the Salvadoran people."[17] The concrete conditions in which the poor live help us grasp the scope of our own conversion to the Lord. As Bishop Leonidas Proaño has put it:

> If conversion should be a turning to God and neighbor, then we must ask ourselves whether we perhaps do not show greater respect to images made of wood than to human beings who are the living images of God. We must ask ourselves whether we are not more courteous to images than to the human beings who are sunk in ignorance, sorrow, poverty, and slavery.[18]

A concern for the material needs of the poor is an element in our spirituality.[19] The sincerity of our conversion to the Lord is to be judged by the action to which this concern leads us. A joint statement of grassroots communities in Managua, Nicaragua, reads in part:

> We committed Christians who sign this document are trying to strip ourselves of the old person and embody in ourselves the new person by following Christ our brother. He rejects (Mk 2:21–22) a spirituality that is nothing but an idealist frame of mind and accepts only one that leads to a commitment to clothing the naked, educating the ignorant, and so on. Today more than ever before the words of Christ have special meaning: what you do to the most wretched you do to me.[20]

There is an echo here, once again, of Matthew 25:31–46. The concrete and definitional character of this passage has long made it play an outstanding role in the spiritual experience of Latin American Christians.[21] The text cannot be properly interpreted except by situating it within the gospel message as a whole. I shall look at other aspects of it further on; for the moment let me emphasize only one of its main thrusts.

The text is one of the many in the gospels that underscores

the importance of action in behalf of the poor in the following of Jesus. But there is something distinctive in the passage
from Matthew: it reminds us that what we do to the poor we
do to Christ himself. It is this fact that gives action in behalf of
the poor its decisive character and prevents it from being taken
simply as an expression of the "social dimension" of faith. No, it
is much more than that; such action has an element of contemplation, of encounter with God, at the very heart of the work
of love. And this encounter is not "merited" by any work; it is
the gratuitous gift of the Lord. This is what the passage in question makes known to us, and in so doing it evokes our surprise
("When did we see you hungry?").

This is a work of love that implies a gift of self and is not
simply a matter of fulfilling a duty. It is a work of concrete,
authentic love for the poor that is not possible apart from a
certain integration into their world and not possible apart from
bonds of real friendship with those who suffer despoliation and
injustice.[22] The solidarity is not with "the poor" in the abstract
but with human beings of flesh and bone. Without love and
affection, without—why not say it?—tenderness, there can be
no true gesture of solidarity. Where these are lacking there is an
impersonality and coldness (however well intentioned and accompanied by a desire for justice) that the flesh-and-blood poor
will not fail to perceive. True love exists only among equals, "for
love effects a likeness between the lover and the object loved."[23]
And this supposes an ability to approach others and respect their
sensitivities.[24]

Consistency and Stubbornness

The new way that we undertake and to which we are constantly being converted calls for constancy and deep conviction:
"At present we are a people that knows only pain. We endure in
darkness, with the stubborn certainty that some day a pure and
free human being and human society will be born."[25]

The stubbornness we often find in the great saints is nothing but the expression of a profound fidelity that does not bow to difficulties and obstacles. A great Chilean bishop, recently deceased, said: "We believe that our identity as Christians and as a church is being purified and deepened by every conflict, provided that we try first and foremost to be faithful to the Spirit of Jesus Christ who is guiding the one history of salvation and integral liberation for the poor and for all humankind."[26]

Spirituality as an all-embracing attitude is precisely a force that bestows constancy and prevents our being "tossed to and fro and carried about with every wind of doctrine" (Eph 4:14). This stubbornness—for that is what I am talking about—has its source in hope, "for we know," as a statement by Guatemalan religious formulates it, "that after the 'torments of unleashed violence' that now afflict us, the sun of justice of God our Father will shine again. We will not betray our cause even though it brings us persecution and death, because we trust that Christ is present in the tragic reality that is our present life."[27]

Hope often finds support in the testimonies of those who have been called to give up their lives. Archbishop Romero, in one of his homilies, said:

> Lord, this day our conversion and faith draw support from those who lie there in their coffins. They are messengers who convey the reality of our people and the noble aspirations of a church that seeks naught but the salvation of the people. See, Lord, the multitude that is gathered in your cathedral is itself the prayer of a people that groans and weeps but does not despair, because it knows that Christ did not lie: the kingdom is indeed at hand and requires only that we be converted and believe in it.[28]

This is the prayer of a pastor and brother who sustains the hope of his people.

In the gospels fear and inconstancy are seen as failures of faith. Jesus' exhortation to his disciples, "Have no fear" (e.g., Mt 14:27), has a positive meaning: have faith, know how to trust. Paul frequently calls upon his communities to "be steadfast in faith." An authentic and solid spirituality will prevent our being easily shaken in our commitments and our Christian life. Teresa of Ávila says of those who would have such steadfastness:

> It is most important—all important, indeed—that they should begin well by making an earnest and most deter- mined resolve not to halt . . . whatever may come, what- ever may happen to them, however hard they may have to labor, whoever may complain of them, whether they reach their goal or die on the road . . . whether the very world dissolves before them.[29]

This "determined resolve" is what I have been calling "stubborn- ness. It is the steadfastness of those who are convinced, those who know what they want, those who put their trust in the Lord and devote their lives to others: "Those who trust in the Lord are like Mount Zion, which cannot be moved, but abides forever" (Ps 125:1).

The solidarity required by the preferential option for the poor forces us back to a fundamental Christian attitude: a grasp of the need for continual conversion. We are then able to find in the break with former ways and in our chosen new way deeper dimensions of a personal and social, material and spiritual, kind. The conversion to the Lord to which solidarity with the op- pressed brings us calls for stubbornness and constancy on the road we have undertaken. . . .

*   *   *

. . . Concern for effective action is a way of expressing love for the other. The gratuitousness of the gift of the kingdom does not do away with effective action but rather calls for it all the more. "In the presence of this God who acts gratuitously we must show society a reign that is not reducible to energy expended in the service of human development, but that has its source in an encounter with a personal God with whom intimacy is bestowed as a *gift* and who, once given to us, neither suppresses nor competes with the human *effort* to build a better world."[30]

It would be easy to conclude, especially in this age of "antidualism," that what is required of us is a synthesis of gratuitousness and effectiveness. There is something to this, but at the same time the subject is more complex and calls for greater discernment. A well-known text from the Ignatian spiritual tradition may offer a fruitful approach: "In matters which he [Ignatius] took up pertaining to the service of our Lord, he made use of all the human means to succeed in them, with a care and efficiency as great as if the success depended on these means; and he confided in God and depended on his providence as greatly as if all the other human means which he was using were of no effect."[31]

What we have here is more than a synthesis. Gratuitousness is an atmosphere in which the entire quest for effectiveness is bathed. It is something both subtler and richer than a balance maintained between two important aspects. This alternative perspective does not represent an abandonment of efficacy but rather seeks to locate efficacy in a comprehensive and fully human context that is in accord with the gospel. That context is the space of freely bestowed encounter with the Lord. A gratuitous encounter is mysterious and it draws us into itself. Many Latin American Christians are attempting to live the gratuitous love of God by committing themselves to a liberative undertaking.

A matter of great importance to the faith arises at this point. Paul, requesting that others in the community (*koinonia*) collaborate "for the poor among the saints at Jerusalem" (Rom 15:26), a task on which he lays great emphasis,[32] writes with tact and clarity: "I say this not as a command, but to prove by the earnestness of others that your love also is genuine" (2 Cor 8:8). There is nothing more urgent than gratitude, for it "proves" that love is "genuine."

Everything Is Grace

The experience and idea of the gratuitousness of God's love are fundamental and of central importance in the Christian life.[33] The gratuitous initiative of the Lord is a dominant theme in Pauline theology ("The free gift in the grace of that one man Jesus Christ abounded for many" (Rom 5:15), as also later in Augustinian theology.

"God first loved us" (1 Jn 4:19). Everything starts from there. The gift of God's love is the source of our being and puts its impress on our lives. We have been made by love and for love. Only by loving, then, can we fulfill ourselves as persons; that is how we respond to the initiative taken by God's love.[34]

God's love for us is gratuitous; we do not merit it. It is a gift we receive before we exist, or, to be more accurate, a gift in view of which we have been created. Election to adoptive filiation comes first:

> Blessed be the God and Father of our Lord Jesus Christ, who has blessed us in Christ with every spiritual blessing in the heavenly places, even as he chose us in him before the foundation of the world, that we should be holy and blameless before him. He destined us in love to be his sons through Jesus Christ, according to the purpose of his will. (Eph 1:3–51)

Gratuitousness thus marks our lives so that we are led to love gratuitously and to want to be loved gratuitously. It is a profoundly human characteristic. Such is our makeup. True love is always a gift, something that transcends motives and merits. As is said so beautifully in the Canticle of Canticles, "Many waters cannot quench love, neither can floods drown it. If a man offered for love all the wealth of his house, it would be utterly scorned"

(8:7). Gratitude is the space of that radical self-giving and that presence of beauty in our lives without which even the struggle for justice would be crippled.[35]

If this is true of human life as a whole, it is particularly true in the matter that concerns us here. The experience of gratuitousness is the space of encounter with the Lord. Unless we understand the meaning of gratuitousness, there will be no contemplative dimension in our life. Contemplation is not a state of paralysis but of radical self-giving. In the final analysis, to believe in God means to live our life as a gift from God and to look upon everything that happens in it as a manifestation of this gift.

In saying all this I am not trying to ignore the coherence proper to history (the realm of what Thomistic theology calls "second causes"). On the contrary, my intention is to penetrate to the deepest meaning of history and, in the words of Ignatius of Loyola, to "find God in all things." But the fact is that the attitude of finding God in all things can be acquired only if we can activate a contemplative dimension in our lives. Contemplation disposes us to recognize that "everything is grace," to use an expression of Bernanos, which in fact comes from Thérèse of Lisieux, who, contrary to the deformed image of her that has long been passed on to us, was indeed a powerful saint.

Prayer is an expression of faith and trust in the Lord; it is an act that is peculiar to and characteristic of the believer. It takes place in the context of the love that we know to be marked in its very source by gratuitousness. Prayer is in fact a loving dialogue, to use the description given by Teresa of Ávila.[36] It arises as a humble and trusting response to the Father's gratuitous gift of love and expresses our desire to share that gift in an unaffected way with our brothers and sisters. Mary's canticle says it well: "My soul magnifies the Lord, and my spirit rejoices in God my Savior, for he has regarded the low estate of his handmaiden" (Lk 1:46–48).

Like every dialogue of love, prayer runs the risk of being interpreted as a "useless activity," whereas in point of fact it is precisely an experience of a gratuitousness that creates new forms of communication. It is expressed, for example, in the silence proper to prayer, as indeed to every loving encounter (human experience bears witness to this). A moment comes when words can no longer communicate the depth of what is experienced. Simple and silent presence is a touchstone of love.

From gratuitousness also comes the language of symbols. The experience of human love leads us to recognize that "rites are necessary," as Antoine de Saint-Exupéry said. We resort to symbols in the liturgy, in community prayer: they move within the ambit of the language of gratuitous love.

Some sectors of the Latin American church are passing through a time of prayer.[37] It is surprising to see a people becoming increasingly better organized and more effective in the struggle to assert its rights to life and justice[38] and at the same time giving evidence of a profound sense of prayer and of a conviction that in the final analysis love and peace are an unmerited gift of God.[39]

In their religious celebrations, whether at especially important moments or in the circumstances of everyday life, the poor turn to the Lord with the trustfulness and spontaneity of a child who speaks to its father and tells him of its suffering and hopes.[40] One Christian community that had suffered a harsh trial writes with simplicity: "We tell all our Christian brothers and sisters that we have the courage to continue to celebrate our faith in groups as often as we can."[41] "As often as we can": the harsh situation in which a people lives forces it to pray "in the catacombs."

A Twofold Movement

Matthew 25:31–46 plays an important part in the Latin American spiritual experience. The passage is a great help in grasping the requirement of effective action in the service of the other. And indeed not only of effective action but also of what we might call the "earthiness" of Christian love, in contrast to a spiritualistic interpretation of that love. The Matthean text makes it easier to understand that encounter with the poor through concrete works is a necessary step in view of encounter with Christ himself.

But we have also come to understand that a true and full encounter with our neighbor requires that we first experience the gratuitousness of God's love. Once we have experienced it, our approach to others is purified of any tendency to impose an alien will on them; it is disinterested and respectful of their personalities, their needs and aspirations. The other is our way for reaching God, but our relationship with God is a precondition for encounter and true communion with the other. It is not possible to separate these two movements, which are perhaps really only a single movement: Jesus Christ, who is God and man, is our way to the Father, but he is also our way to recognition of others as brothers and sisters.[42] The experience of the gratuitousness of God's love—which is a basic datum of the Christian faith—is not simply a kind of historical parenthesis as it were; rather it gives human becoming its full meaning. A realization of this is gradually becoming a basic element in the spiritual experience now coming into existence in Latin America.

I am aware of the limitations of what I have been saying. The experience is not universal, nor is it always explicit, nor, on the other hand, is it entirely new. Moreover, an inevitable inertia is still with us. Nonetheless, a significant dynamism is clearly forming. The experience of gratuitousness is not a form of evasion but rather the locus of life and the reality that envelops and permeates the endeavor to achieve historical efficacy. This efficacy will be sought with ever-increasing fervor in the measure that it reveals to us the gratuitous love of God: God's preference for the poor.

A commitment that takes shape in effective action is therefore required by the gratuitous love of the Lord, but let us not forget that an inverse moment is also needed: the contemplation that historical action calls for.[43]

—*Translated by Matthew J. O'Connell*

Notes

[1] See Gustavo Gutiérrez, *A Theology of Liberation: History, Politics, and Salvation,* trans. and ed. by Sister Caridad Inda and John Eagleson (1973; Maryknoll, NY: Orbis Books, 1988), 205: "Evangelical conversion is indeed the touchstone of all spirituality. Conversion means a radical transformation of ourselves; it means thinking, feeling, and living as Christ—present in exploited and alienated man."

[2] R. Schnackenburg, *Christian Existence in the New Testament* (Notre Dame, IN: University of Notre Dame Press, 1968), 1:36: "We turn back from the wrong direction and take a new route."

[3] Pastoral ministers, priests, religious women, and pastors of Bolivia, January 20, 1973, in *Praxis del martirio ayer y hoy* (Bogotá: CEPLA, 1977), 125–26. Or again: "In view of the fact that we ought to be engaged in struggle and in view of the suffering of our people, individualism, fearfulness, and cowardice are sins" (from the Fourth Meeting of the Christians of Puno [Peru], 1980; text published in RIMAC, the documentation service of the Instituto Bartolomé de Las Casas).

[4] One example: "The luxury of a few becomes an insult to the wretched poverty of the vast masses. This is contrary to the plan of the Creator and to the honor that is due him. In this anxiety and sorrow the church sees a situation of social sinfulness, all the more serious because it exists in countries that call themselves Catholic and are capable of changing the situation" (Puebla Document ["Final Document of the Third General Conference of the Latin American Episcopate"], in *Puebla and Beyond,* ed. John Eagleson and Philip Scharper [Maryknoll, NY: Orbis Books, 1979], 122–285, no. 28).

[5] "She (the Virgin Mary) makes it possible for us to overcome the manifold 'structures of sin' in which our lives—personal, familial, and social—are encased. She makes it possible for us to obtain the grace of true liberation—the liberation by which Christ has liberated humankind in its entirety" (homily in the Shrine of Our Lady of Zapopan, no. 3).

[6] "Evangelización: Algunas lineas pastorales," in *Documentos del episcopado: La Pastoral conciliar en el Perú en la Iglesia 1968–1977* (Lima: EAPSA, 1979), 185.

[7] Pastoral exhortation in *Boletín del arzobispado* (October 1978), 36.

[8] Homily on February 16, 1979. In the same perspective the Episcopal Conference of El Salvador wrote in its message of March 5, 1977: "This is the fundamental sin that we pastors must denounce. There can be no ignoring of the people or playing with it and its hopes. As long as no determined and effective effort is made to solve the problems of the distribution of wealth and land, of participation in government, and of the organization of rural and urban inhabitants, their status as citizens and children of God is being ignored" (in *Signos de vida y fidelidad: Testimonios de la Iglesia en América latina, 1978–1982* [Lima: CEP, 1983] 275a; hereafter *SVF*).

[9] "It has been said that interior conversion does not suffice, that we are held to perfect and progressively reconquer our entire being for God. Today we must be aware that what we must reconquer and reform is our entire world. In other words, personal conversion and structural reform cannot be separated" (Pedro Arrupe, in *Vie chrétienne,* 178 [June 1975]).

[10] Archbishop Oscar Romero, address at Louvain University (February 2, 1980), in *SVF,* 372a.

[11] "Declaración" (September 5, 1971), in *Signos de lucha y esperanza: Testimonios de la Iglesia en América latina, 1973–1978* (Lima: CEP, 1978), 57a; hereafter *SLE.*

[12] "Unidos en la esperanza" (July 25, 1976), in *SLE,* 86a. Here is another and similar passage: "It cannot be denied that the church and Christians are passing through a painful but real process of conversion. Since Vatican II and more particularly since Medellín, they have been becoming more aware of the radical no that God says to our sins of omission. In a greater or lesser degree we have set about collaborating for a more human society that, as we Christians see it, means the approach of the reign of God" (Episcopal Conference of El Salvador, March 5, 1977, in *SLE,* 181b).

[13] Vicaría de la Solidaridad de Santiago, Chile, "Abrir la huella del Buen Samaritano" (1976), in *SLE,* 140a.

[14] See the encyclical *On Human Work* in which the church is called to solidarity with the just claims of worker movements (no. 8).

[15] See G. Thils, *Théologie des réalités terrestres* (Bruges: Desclée de Brouwer, 1946), vol. 1.

[16] This is in agreement with Berdyaev's statement: "If I am hungry, that is a material problem; if someone else is hungry, that is a spiritual problem."

[17] R. Grande, a Jesuit priest murdered in El Salvador, homily at Apopa (February 13, 1971), in *SLE,* 260a. See Martin Lange and Reinhold Iblacker, eds., *Witnesses of Hope,* translated from the German by William E. German (Maryknoll, NY: Orbis, 1981), 27–33.

[18] "Cuaresma y conversión" (March 10, 1972), in *SLE,* 272a.

[19] Pope John Paul II, writing on the spirituality of work, says: "The entire human person, body and spirit, participates in work, whether it be manual or intellectual. And the word of the living God, the gospel of salvation, is addressed not to a part of the human being, but the entirety" (*On Human Work,* no. 24).

[20] In *Nicaragua a un año de la victoria,* ed. Ana Gispert-Sauch (Lima: CEP, 1980), 72.

[21] Since the sixteenth century the situation of poverty and oppression of the Amerindians has turned their defenders to this gospel text. And it inspired the celebrated expression of Bartolomé de Las Casas—the "flogged Christs of the Indies." The Amerindian, Guamán Poma, has said, with deep biblical rootage: "It seems to the rich and haughty that where a poor person is, God and justice are not. But it must be understood in the faith that where a poor

person is, there is Jesus Christ; and where God is, there is justice" (*Nueva corónica* [Mexico City: Siglo Veintiuno, 1980), 2:903).

²² Where such bonds exist, the lowly open their world to all those who are in solidarity with them. At the burial of Father Vicente Hondarza (of Huacho, Peru), who died under circumstances that have never been explained, a *campesino* said: "For us field-workers it is hard to express what the physical absence of Fr. Vicente means. He was a priest who understood the meaning of the church, a priest who shared his life working with the neediest, always bringing the gospel message to the poor, to those in need, to workers in the fields. We are saddened because we have lost a beloved companion" (in *Páginas* 54 [1983]: 31). In a similar vein Bishop Martín Zegarra, the bishop of Santiago de Veraguas, Panama, wrote after the disappearance of Father Héctor Gallego: "I assure you, Héctor, that we think about you, that we love you, that we admire what you did for the poor, the needy, those who are the object of God's predilection, of our Father who is the Truth and who wants us to search the truth in full and live an authentic freedom. Do you know what, Héctor? I cannot believe that you will not return" (1971, in *Signos de liberación: Testimonios de la Iglesia en América latina, 1969–1973* (Lima: CEP, 1973), 68; hereafter *SL*).

²³ St. John of the Cross, *Ascent of Mount Carmel,* 1, 4, 3, in *The Collected Works of St. John of the Cross,* trans. Kieran Kavanaugh and Otilio Rodriguez (Garden City, NY: Doubleday, 1964; paperback reprint: Washington, DC: Institute of Carmelite Studies, 1973), 78.

²⁴ As Paul did and his letters show: "God is my witness, how I yearn for you all with the affection of Christ Jesus" (Phil 1:8).

²⁵ A group of Chilean Christians, November 1973, in *SLE,* 9b.

²⁶ Bishop Enrique Alvear, "La toma en Pudahuel y el drama de las familias sin casa" (1981), in *SVF,* 188b.

²⁷ Statement of the Conference of Religious of Guatemala regarding the problems of El Quiché (August 1980), in *SVF,* 441b.

²⁸ Homily of January 21, 1979.

²⁹ Teresa of Ávila, *The Way of Perfection* (New York: Sheed & Ward, 1946; Image Books, 1964), 150. For a brief presentation of the witness of Teresa of Ávila, see Marla del Carmen Diez, "Teresa de Ávila doctora de la experiencia," in *Páginas* 40 (September 1981): 10–14. In language free of cliché Christian *campesino* remarked at a gathering: "I believe that the reign of God exists right in the harsh life of the people, because there are many weaknesses, aren't there? Sometimes a man gets weary, but something gives him a push. Then it is in the very strength of the people that the reign of God is to be found" (fourth meeting of the Christians of Puno, 1980). "Something gives him a push" and keeps him from drawing back.

³⁰ CLAR (Latin American Conference of Religious), *Documento de la IV Asamblea General* (December 1969), in *SL,* 279a.

[31] In J. de Guibert, *The Jesuits, Their Spiritual Doctrine and Practice: A Historical Study* (Chicago: Institute of Jesuit Sources, 1964), 148n55. There are several versions of this Ignatian maxim. I have cited the one that goes back to Pedro Ribadaneira and is to be found in the *Monumenta Ignatiana*. For a penetrating, though at times somewhat forced, study of this and similar formulations, see G. Fessard, *La dialectique des Exercices spirituels de Saint Ignace de Loyola* (Paris: Aubier, 1966), 1:303–63.

[32] See L. Cerfaux, *L'itinéraire spirituel de saint Paul* (Paris: Cerf, 1966), 132–35. For the ecclesiological implications of *koinonia,* see M. Legido López, *Fraternidad en el mundo* (Salamanca: Sígueme, 1982), esp. 209–86.

[33] See Gutiérrez, *Theology of Liberation,* 205–6: "A spirituality of liberation must be filled with a living sense of *gratuitousness.* Communion with the Lord and with all men is more than anything else a gift. . . . The knowledge that at the root of our personal and community existence lies the gift of the self-communication with God, the grace of his friendship, fills our life with gratitude."

[34] See H. Echegaray, "Conocer a Dios es practicar la justicia," in *Anunciar el Reino* (Lima: CEP, 1981): "The measure of our fidelity depends not on the native capacities of our own hearts but on the abundant gifts that the Lord bestows on us. The word of God awakens profound and unforeseeable energies."

[35] This is the insight possessed by many who are committed to this struggle. Juan Gonzalo Rose, in exile for political reasons, has said it beautifully in a poem to his sister (*Carta a María Teresa*):

> I ask myself now
> why I do not limit my love
> to the sudden roses,
> the tides of June,
> the moons over the sea?
> Why have I had to love
> the rose *and* justice,
> the sea *and* justice,
> justice *and* the light?

The same testimony is given by the lowly but heroic people of Nicaragua, a people of poets who are able to combine constancy in defending their right to life and dignity with the cultivation of beauty in song and poetry.

[36] In her *Life,* chap. 8, in *The Collected Works of St. Teresa of Ávila,* trans. Kieran Kavanaugh and Otilio Rodriguez (Washington, DC: Institute of Carmelite Studies, 1976), vol. 1.

[37] See the interesting anthology of prayers composed in Latin America compiled by Charles Antoine, *L'Amérique latine en priére* (Paris: Cerf, 1981).

³⁸ On this point, see Juan Hernandez Pico, "La oración en los procesos lati-noamericanos de liberación," in *Espiritualidad de la liberación,* ed. A. Cussiánovich et al. (Lima: CEP, 1980), 159–85; and Frei Betto, "Oração, exigencia (tambem) política," *Revista Eclesiástica Brasileira* 42 (1982): 444–55.

³⁹ Henri Nouwen, after a stay in Bolivia and Peru, has written that there he learned how to say *gracias,* "thanks." The familiar expression *demos gracias* ("let us give thanks") became for him something more than a prayer said before eating: he now understands it in the sense of projecting the whole of life in the presence of God and all God's people in an atmosphere of gratitude (*Gracias: A Latin American Journal* [San Francisco: Harper & Row, 1983], 187).

⁴⁰ I offer as an example the following prayer in which Bishop José Dammen sums up the feelings of his people: "Lord, the men and women of the Andes cry to you because of the utter poverty in which we live, subject to the vagaries of nature and even more to oppression by other human beings. With resignation and patience and while contemplating the sorrowful passion of your Son as an image of our own sufferings, we have for centuries endured the scarcity of food and the lack of work for a large majority of our young who have no alternatives but wretchedness and delinquency. There is no future for them on a tiny parcel of land that is exhausted by millennia of tilling. The fruit of our labor in fields and mines is appropriated by others who leave us but a few crumbs. Necessity compels us men and women of the Andes to toil from childhood on, and the harshness of our life leaves us no respite.

"We know, nonetheless, that you are a God of mercy and that you take pity on the needy. Therefore we renew our cries—often in silence like Mary at the foot of the cross—from the depths of our hearts. We adore your providence and we intensify our hope of the human fellowship that your Christ teaches us and that we practice with generous hospitality" (*Veinticinco años al servicio de la Iglesia* [Lima: CEP, 1983], 248–49).

⁴¹ Letter from the communities of El Quiché, January 1981, after the massacre in that part of Guatemala and the forced withdrawal of the bishop and pastoral ministers, in *Morir y despertar en Guatemala* (Lima: CEP, 1981), 144. The same attitude finds expression in this prayer of Luis Espinal, a Jesuit priest murdered in Bolivia: "Lord of mystery, let us feel your presence at the heart of life; we desire to find you in the depths of everyday things" (*Oraciones a Quemarropa* [Lima: CEP, 1982], 32).

⁴² Gutiérrez, *Theology of Liberation,* 206–7.

⁴³ This is why some have now been paraphrasing the well-known "contemplative in action" of Ignatian spirituality and speaking of "contemplatives in political action" in action that change history. See G. Gutiérrez, "Praxis de liberación y fe cristiana," in *SL,* p. 24; L. Boff, "Contemplativus in liberatione," in Cussiánovich, *Espiritualidad de la liberación* (Lima: CEP, 1982), 119.

5

Conversion in the Time of Cholera

A Reflection on Structural Violence and Social Change

Paul Farmer

One of the benefits of working on this book has been the chance to continue a conversation with Gustavo Gutiérrez. Another has been revisiting his work (the way in which so many have had conversations with him over the past several decades). I was asked by the architect-editors of this book to comment on a specific essay, Chapter 6 of *We Drink from Our Own Wells*, Father Gutiérrez's best-known book on the link between spirituality and social justice.

The chapter is called "Conversion: A Requirement for Solidarity," and I first read it almost twenty-five years ago. It's not the essay I'd have chosen on my own, and rereading it a quarter of a century later, not in Haiti or Peru but in Rwanda, raises several challenges for me. The first is obvious and temporal: the reader (and the author) are different from the people we were decades ago, though the text on the printed page stays the same. This sort of interpretive challenge is second nature to theologians and literary critics but less familiar terrain to many others. I've had the great privilege, during the years elapsed between my two readings of this chapter, to work in some of the countries mentioned in Gutiérrez's writings. These places have changed, too, as has the rest of the continent on which Gutiérrez was raised, as has the continent where he did some of his studies, and as has the one from which I write now.

Places and people always change. But there are continuities as well, and these inform the metaphor of his title, the wells dug deep in time and space, deep into lands stretching from Peru to Brazil and Chile, from Guatemala to El Salvador. If any place is spiritually significant to Gutiérrez's work, that place must be Latin America, which he sees as inhabited by people intimately and culturally related to one another, though diverse. Hence the curious subtitle of the book: "The Spiritual Journey of a People." Tensions between timeless truths and rapid social change, between the large scale and the local, between the general and the specific, inform Gutiérrez's reflections on poverty and the struggle against it. Engaging in this struggle is of course what he means by "solidarity."

The next set of interpretive challenges pertains to the relationship between diverse notions of conversion and of social change, and I will take a detour to discuss the latter first. This is not to say that sociological understanding and some rudimentary knowledge of political economy are all that is requisite to understand either spirituality or solidarity, an assertion that Gutiérrez and others have termed a "caricature" of liberation theology. It is, rather, modesty about theology, a field in which I've not been trained, and a chance to draw on two fields in which I have: not sociology or political economy, but clinical medicine and anthropology. Both the practice of medicine and the discipline of anthropology offer insights into this chapter from *Wells* and on much of Gutiérrez's work.[1]

Drawing on one's own training to reflect on other fields of knowledge is hardly novel—liberation theology was born, after all, out of linking theological reflection to insights coming from research in several other disciplines—nor are such epistemological exercises as important as considering personal *experiences* of struggling against poverty.[2] To contextualize Gutiérrez's work, I draw on my own experience seeking to provide, along with many others, medical care in settings of rural poverty and among the poor and marginalized in urban settings in which affluence and penury are hard against one another; but most of all, I draw on the experience of patients (and they do term themselves patients) facing both poverty and disease.

Processual Understandings of Conversion and Social Change

Although specialists in any field are rankled by simplifications, I will risk saying that most liberation theologians seek to root their own reflections and understanding not only in the specifics of place but also in time. When Father Gutiérrez acknowledges a time—the "new" of which he writes in *Wells*—it's the 1960s and after. His project was born of a strong identification with the liberation and social-justice struggles of late twentieth-century Latin America, which took the lives of several of his friends and acquaintances (and many thousands of others) but which also breathed life into a somewhat rigid Catholic Church. Of course, institutions also change, since they are as rooted in context as the people who create and maintain and transform them. But the Latin American church was seen by many as inflexible and unchanging (*viz.*, "rigid") because it fit too neatly into an ostensibly static social order in which a few had much and most had far too little. It was this neat fit that led Archbishop Oscar Romero and many others to push the church toward what they saw as its original role: to side with the poor and oppressed in the struggle against their own poverty, to break with the past and present, and to create a new community in which justice might prevail along with the corporal works of mercy. A similar wind blew through the church in Brazil and across the continent, and thence around the world in different ways and times.

I witnessed some of these transformations in Haiti after the fall of the Duvalier dictatorship, which occurred in 1986. I was then a student of medicine and anthropology at Harvard, spending

part of each year in rural Haiti. Many testimonies about this period have been written in French, and some in Haitian Creole.
Amy Wilentz wrote a remarkable account of these stormy years,
The Rainy Season: Haiti since Duvalier, even as these events were
unfolding. Her first-person account suggests how the church
there was renewed—shaken, in the views of some—by these
transformations.[3] Although I followed them more than did most
students of medicine or anthropology, my readings were not in
ecclesiology and very rarely in theology: they were, rather, non-
specialist books like Wilentz's or Penny Lernoux's *People of God,*[4]
or the emerging ethnographic works on these changes.[5] Being
in Haiti during this time—specifically, as a young American student—taught me that social change is never experienced the
same way by any two people and that the sharpest differences in
experience were those across social classes.

From my first week in Haiti, I could observe what Amy Wilentz would later call the "giant hideous gaping crevasse" between
my world and that of the Haitians.[6] But what I didn't expect (as
a twenty-three-year-old American) was the experientially near,
and thus palpable, nature of the crevasse separating rich and poor
Haitians. Conversations in a rural squatter settlement in central Haiti often turned to deploring the fecklessness of the rich
(with the Creole versions of the words "rich" and "bourgeois"
used unstintingly to describe the nonpoor, most of whom were
neither rich nor bourgeois by any of the standard definitions)
and the unmerited misfortunes of the poor. The stuffy consulta-
tion rooms of the small clinic we built there and the courtyard
outside echoed with lament and much "God-talk," to use one of
Gutiérrez's terms. Things will never change, I heard.

But they did change. The ostensibly rigid dictatorship was
revealed to be fragile, as such arrangements so often are, when it
tottered and fell within a few months of a series of "food riots"
that began in 1985 in the poorest parts of the restive city of Gonaïves.[7] These protests were a response not only to a sharp rise
in food prices but to the increasing food insecurity that Haitians
faced as their own agricultural sector faltered as a consequence

of "free trade." The terms of the informal theodicy I was hearing as my hosts and patients explained their misfortunes were also changing rapidly.[8] This was true not only in discussions of illness but also of what were termed "neoliberal policies" that weakened Haitian farmers unable to compete with cheaper goods from their larger neighbor to the north, with its mechanized farming and agricultural subsidies.

Despite visible changes and new freedoms to imagine a different world, the abysses were not readily bridged. Deciphering social change (or process) became a national preoccupation, along with dread of the converse, stagnation and stasis.

I found myself in that liminal state, which both anthropologists and doctors seek, of trying to see events and processes from several points of view at once. For anthropologists, the messy details of everyday life and personal experience are considered central to ethnographic understanding; a physician is expected to elicit patients' views and experiences and also to understand pathophysiologic processes that are seen everywhere and are the reason why an x-ray or a laboratory result, or a surgical procedure, are not so dissimilar or context-specific that a radiologist or a pathologist or a surgeon trained in Boston would be of no use in Haiti. This early experience in Haiti was sometimes painful, often confusing, and, more than occasionally, illuminating. It certainly marked and changed me.

Addressing this suffering led us, slowly but surely, to draw on liberation theology but also to interrogate claims of causality about suffering (in theodicy, say) with the help of those affected directly by poverty and disease and thus experts on such matters. The importance of this approach was underlined, again and again, by the anthropologists, whose reliance on local knowledge sometimes bordered on the pathological, but also by the theologians and historians I was then reading. Direct experience with certain events (an illness, say, or an epidemic, but also a coup d'état or a hurricane or a food riot) could be useful. But it would not always explain the *origins* of suffering, which was rarely if ever the result of happenstance. This was true even in times of rapid social change. In other words, I learned early to be wary of what some historians term the "event-focused" interpretation of change and to return, again and again, to process and structure. Both process and structure are terms invented to remind us that, when contemplating social suffering, both problems and solutions are fundamentally social ones.

Gutiérrez also acknowledges that the word "conversion" (like others he uses often, including "break" and "irruption") signals a process as often as it does an event. Understanding discontinuity calls for shared reflection more than personal epiphany. For Gutiérrez the theologian and priest, this reflection was informed by his studies; by his own family's experience, growing up poor in urban Peru; by working with parish families in similar or worse circumstances; and by seeking to re-frame, whether in Lima or Medellín or Puebla, his church's role in this struggle. Spirituality is always social. Gutiérrez's life and work remind us that the hard grind of making a preferential option for the poor is necessarily done with others and is always more than a personal project affecting some strictly interior "spiritual life."

In the face of social injustice, de-socialized views of spirituality are sometimes revealed as an illusion.[9] But when are we not in the face of injustice simply because injustice is not, to use American slang, in our face? The suffering generated by extreme poverty was the result not of happenstance or lack of industry among the poor, but rather generated by institutions and conditions that were and are of human making. That's why some of my Harvard teachers, including anthropologist-physician Arthur Kleinman, used the term *social suffering* to describe the lot of those marginalized by poverty, racism, gender inequality, or a toxic admixture of these and other forces and events, including war and slavery and political violence.[10] Since such social suffering is only rarely local in terms of its causes, didn't that mean that any spirituality or moral philosophy informed by the suffering of others requires an awareness of injustice, whether in view or hidden away, as Gutiérrez and his peers claimed?[11] This was also, essentially, the claim of my Haitian teachers (hosts and friends and patients), whose vigorously socialized theodicy further interrogated this illusion. In their experience, most suffering was caused by the actions of others, as slavery and (more recently) dictatorship had been, rather than by drought or storm or other *force majeure* beyond human control.[12]

Yet the illusion of natural, rather than social, causation often prevails wherever social injustice does; contradictory claims of causality about poverty and social suffering were rooted in these and other mystifications encountered in settings across time and space. My rural Haitian acquaintances thus implicitly echoed old-school political economists who made confident claims of causality regarding social and cultural constructs and their relationship to economic institutions.[13] Such constructs were not "natural" but rather the result, whether as prop or resistance, of unequal economic institutions.

In the midst of ideological debates about the various "isms" and of wars hot and cold arose another claim, more humbly advanced: there are many ways to fight poverty and to promote just development, but improving the lives of the poor, right here and now, is too often forgotten. One of the reasons Gutiérrez's work names persistent poverty and growing social inequalities as "scandalous," a recurrent term in his work, is that he and others sought to change, or convert, common notions of scandal. Poverty is, he averred, not only the ranking spiritual problem of our times but also its greatest scandal. This view from below, as opposed to any one philosophical or political framework, always informs his work.[14]

For a medical student working in Haiti, one with only the most rudimentary notion of theology, Gutiérrez's message was an exhortation to work with those seeking to provide basic services, especially medical care, to some of the most oppressed people in Latin America. Throughout these years, our pragmatic efforts to bring medical and social services to the poor, carried out by people with different and complementary motivations, were inspired and informed by the theologian from Peru and by others, in Haiti and elsewhere. Colleagues who lacked familiarity or interest in theology, Catholic or otherwise, were inspired by the notion of a "preferential option for the poor in health care." And so we claimed it as our mission, rather than some totalizing framework for solving all the world's ills.[15] (I've laid out one account of how this synergy informed the work of Partners In Health in Chapters 1 and 3 of this volume, the former a doctor's tribute to the theologian.)

This synergy also informed my doctoral dissertation, which was based on work done in Haiti during those turbulent years at the end of the 1980s, and subsequent work in medicine and anthropology. The subjective sense of events and temporality, more the focus of historians and historiographers, became one of the topics of my dissertation, which was informed by what one of my thesis advisors had helpfully termed "processual ethnography."[16] This research focused on linking an understanding of the political economy of epidemic disease to local understandings of misfortune (perhaps this should be called "cultural theodicy"?), and made frequent reference to Gutiérrez's writings on what I took to be a closely related topic.[17] Thus did the rural Haitians— with their turbulence and God-talk, their suffering and jeremiads, their vivid history and ways of recounting it—become part of my own conversion, informing my medical practice but also my understanding of both suffering and responses to it. And so did the rural Haitians introduce me, as if for the very first time, to the Catholic social teachings that had seemed so dry and uninteresting to me in my childhood.

The rural Haitians taught me to understand that misfortune, including epidemics, would recur. Nothing about the cholera epidemic now unfolding in Haiti and beyond might be reasonably termed a surprise, as we noted within days of the first Haitian cases. The conversion, to a broad and contextual understanding of social suffering, had occurred decades previously.

From Haiti to Peru:
Cost-effectiveness and "the House of No"

If conversion is a process, rooted in time and place and in so-cial change, it stands to reason that our claims of causality about it should be modest and subject to revision. This is true in large part because most grand efforts to do better in attempts to lessen structural violence are mere essays in the craft: falling off of a horse on the road to Damascus is surely as much a relevant meta-phor as is drinking from a well.

Most germane to me and to others increasingly aware of the complexity of modern poverty was getting to know the people whose spiritual journey was invoked in the subtitle of *Wells* and also its author. This latter acquaintance came to pass because hap-penstance—it would be termed "serendipity" if some of the events that followed were not so tragic—took us to Peru. By 1994, with colleagues including Jim Yong Kim and Jaime Bayona and Father John Roussin and students, I was lucky enough to be working in the dusty slums—*invasiones,* as they were termed—in northern Lima. Poor neighborhoods reaching from the coast and into the hills as flimsy shantytowns were experiencing difficult times: the tail end of a civil war and also the end of an explosive cholera epidemic, which signaled a lack of basic services such as po-table water and modern sanitation and medical care. Once again, any conversion required was one related to the nature of causal claims. As the cholera bacterium spread over Peru and across Latin America, it made its own grim preferential option for the poor. But why were the poor—the "people" in popular parlance and in Gutiérrez's work—at increased risk while the greater citi-zenry was not? Who and which institutions were responsible for mitigating risk?

It was the contention of many, including Father Roussin and new friends and co-workers in Peru, that this epidemic under-lined the failure of governments to provide these services but also the power of community organizing to slow and then stop public-health threats such as cholera. As in Haiti, the Peruvians I met engaged in a lot of God-talk and plenty of focus on the here and now. Our understanding of these threats, from epidemic disease to unemployment, was of course colored by the fact that we worked with Father Roussin and those drawn to this work by liberation theology and by the fact that we worked in the urban Peruvian equivalent of a squatter settlement. Many members of these communities identified strongly as "the organized poor." Many of them sunk their energies into local ("community-based" was the emerging term) efforts to prevent cholera and to save lives even as movement leaders pushed the government, local and national, to invest in municipal water systems so that nothing of the sort would occur in the future. The debate was conflictual and fraught for all of the usual reasons, but also because it occurred during the last years of a civil war in Peru. These were precisely the years in which we began our work in the informal settlements growing in the northern reaches of Lima.

These years were also marked, although we didn't yet know it, by an epidemic of multidrug-resistant tuberculosis ("MDRTB" in the jargon) that in 1995 claimed the life of our friend Father Roussin, not to mention untold hundreds of others in Lima. It's not clear exactly when this epidemic started. But by 1990, drug-resistant tuberculosis affected entire families, spreading quickly and at the time undetected (most infections were followed by what is termed a latent stage) through the air in crowded homes and neighborhoods.

I use the year 1990, even though it's clear that the problems began long before that year, to note two things: first, that most of these patients were infected before our first visits to Peru, and second, that there was nothing new about problems such as MDRTB in cosmopolitan places such as Lima.

Lethal urban epidemics of highly drug-resistant tuberculosis had already been registered in New York and in other (maybe most) megacities. My colleagues and I had seen and documented the first few cases of drug-resistant tuberculosis in rural Haiti, and struggled to diagnose and treat them. Some people died as we were attempting, sometimes in vain, to confirm the diagnosis or to obtain access to effective therapy, which included the same drugs that had been used in New York. But they hadn't been available in Haiti; these medications were also unavailable to the Peruvians who relied on the public-sector tuberculosis clinics, which delivered the great majority of care for tuberculosis free of charge to the patients, even though such treatment was available, if haltingly so, to those able to pay for it. Now, in Peru, we'd just lost a friend and co-worker—one of the founders of Partners In Health—to MDRTB. We had also documented many other "transregional cases" linking the poor parts of Lima to the wealthy ones and linking Peru to the rest of the world. That's how the political economy worked; that's how epidemic disease worked, too.

In short, nothing would have excused our inaction.

But what, exactly, was to be done? We weren't the only ones asking this question. We soon became close to other families already decimated, to use the term technically, by tuberculosis and whose surviving members were sick. By the time the New York epidemic was brought to heel, we were face-to-face (with all that implies, as far as shared risk goes) with patients already sick with the disease in Lima, one of the largest cities in Latin America. Influential policy experts, reflecting a paradigm common in what was then termed international health, claimed that it was not "cost-effective" to try to cure MDRTB in settings of poverty; even trying to do so would be ill-advised and irresponsible.[18] MDRTB thus was deemed "untreatable" in settings of poverty.

These claims troubled us greatly, since they could be made about most diseases, from well-recognized pathologies, such as diabetes or pediatric leukemia, to newer ones, such as AIDS, which in those very years was transformed, in places like Boston or New York, from invariably fatal to chronic and treatable. Declaring an illness "untreatable" in one corner of a globalized economy while treating it in another required a curiously bounded understanding of cost-effectiveness. Such a declaration also seemed to be an illusion, one hard to sustain when considering cholera or any other communicable (and thus transregional) disease. It seemed particularly ill-advised when contemplating an airborne epidemic.[19]

The New York outbreak, which began at the close of the 1970s, was stopped by massive investments in infection control, laboratories, and correctly chosen and assiduously administered treatment. Clinical experts learned, there and elsewhere, that drug-resistant tuberculosis was costly and grueling to treat with the few drugs still effective against these strains. But it worked. It was effective.

If it was effective, how much did it cost? An enormous amount, in terms of lives and treasure, but the exact cost was not held to be as important, it would seem, as effectiveness. Such is the argument of the most important assessment of the costs of the New York epidemic. The part about the cost-effectiveness of these interventions must not have been closely read, since cost and effectiveness, though much discussed, are never really linked together in causal ways. Indeed, they are explicitly dissociated:

> The costs of the resurgence of tuberculosis have been phenomenal. From 1979 through 1994, there were more than 20,000 excess cases of the disease in New York City—cases that would not have occurred if previous downward trends had continued. Each case cost more than $20,000 in 1990 dollars, for a total exceeding $400 million. In addition, as many as one third of patients with tuberculosis were rehospitalized because of inadequate follow-up, and thousands of people were hospitalized in order to rule out the diagnosis. There were additional expenditures for renovation at Rikers Island (more than $60 million); the renovation of hospitals; and preventive therapy for those who became infected during the resurgence. Care will be required for those who become ill, some of them with multidrug-resistant disease, in the years and decades to

come. These costs easily exceed $1 billion and may reach several times that amount. *Thus, despite their cost, efforts to control tuberculosis in the United States are likely to be highly cost effective.*[20]

I've added the italics, of course, because this is not only an influential paper but also one that reveals much about the social construction of causality and of effectiveness and cost. Consider the unlikely (some would say absurd) conclusion: "despite" cost, an intervention is "likely to be highly cost effective." How can something be deemed cost-effective no matter what the cost? Only if the setting in which the intervention takes place has a very high ceiling to acceptable cost within the public sector, as is true in some wealthy countries? Or if the value of human life is genuinely regarded as too valuable or too difficult to value in New York *regardless* of whether the life in question, once imperiled in that city, is from Brooklyn or Manhattan or of Haitian or Peruvian or Cambodian or other origin (most tuberculosis patients in New York and other large coastal cities are foreign born)?

In a sense, this was bracing and affirming to read in Peru, which is where we read it during the very year Father Roussin and others we knew died of the same disease. The debate and the anxiety and friction were really about money for poor people: treatment was deemed "not cost-effective" because there wasn't enough money in the public-health system and not because the best treatment was ineffective. The same argument could be and was made regarding infection control and other preventive measures. Although the city of Lima might not have been able to invest a billion dollars in tuberculosis control, those already sick in Lima and elsewhere in Peru had ample reason to hope that their doctors and nurses did not too readily concede this argument.

The argument could of course not be conceded for any individual or group professing to make a preferential option for the poor in health care. Just as it had done in contemporary theology, an option for the poor turned the usual order upside down in contemplating a new and complex problem, such as highly drug-resistant tuberculosis. This burdensome but rewarding approach to the delivery of health care required not just passion (a prerequisite, perhaps, to all forms of conversion) but also hard-nosed analysis. Who gets sick, and why? Who is spared? What measures might render the poor and vulnerable less so, breaking the cycle of poverty and disease? How best to address the problems of those already sick, to cure their illnesses or palliate their suffering? To protect their families and caregivers and co-workers, and all those who breathed the same air?

The approach was needed and burdensome because it also required a break (conversion) from a past in which access to health care was determined largely by the ability to pay for it. The commodification of health care was widespread across Latin America, including Haiti, as it was and is in the United States.[21] Peru was no exception, as far as most social services were concerned.

Diagnosis and care for drug-resistant tuberculosis was a case in point. It is true that Peru had recently established a competent national tuberculosis program. Peruvians were not supposed to pay for "regular" (*viz.*, drug-susceptible) tuberculosis diagnosis or treatment. In Lima, as in New York and elsewhere, this airborne disease had been declared a *public* health problem and its diagnosis and care were not meant to incur out-of-pocket expense. Such services were for the benefit of all.[22] But the architects of the national program had not anticipated the impact, on certain families in Lima and beyond, of already circulating drug-resistant strains. Until these strains were considered part of the tuberculosis problem, and not dismissed as untreatable or otherwise beyond control, poor families facing such misfortune saw their meager assets and savings frittered away in private clinics and hospitals without access to the "delivery platforms" (to use the jargon of the day) required to address both the disease and the social suffering it engendered.

The country's economic growth, already under way, would result, we suspected, in a smaller burden of tuberculosis as more and more Peruvians were lifted out of poverty. Most patients did just fine once diagnosed with tuberculosis, since the public-sector program gave them a diagnosis and what they needed for cure. But families afflicted with MDRTB saw their economic and social progress halted, and then reversed. In Peru as in most countries, catastrophic illness was the leading cause of tipping people from poverty into destitution, well below the first rung of the ladder leading out of misery.[23] Moreover, these patients knew as well as we did that the disease was spreading to others in their homes and neighborhoods. The experience was hardly less difficult for our Peruvian colleagues (doctors, nurses, community health workers), caught as they were between the patients and the health authorities of their own country. Thus even a well-intentioned social program failed to serve—said no to—some of those whose need of it was greatest. Thus did international health, once a great force for health equity, become "the house of no."

We soon met hundreds, then thousands, of patients needing care for MDRTB and entered into their suffering as best we could. It was unsettling for us and hellish for them, since most had received years of ineffective therapy prior to starting treatment that stood a decent chance of curing them. The treatment we prescribed, though just as good or better than that they'd have received in New York, took two long years to complete, and its side effects were difficult to tolerate. Some died along the way, waiting for treatment or starting too late. Most were cured.[24]

But a small nongovernmental organization such as the nascent Socios En Salud, as the Peruvian branch of Partners In Health was called, could do very little alone; hence the name. Effective solutions would require the creation of broad partnerships designed to address the host of ills ("syndemics" in the words of one of my colleagues)[25] that so often complicate the care of patients living with both chronic disease and poverty. These social afflictions ranged from joblessness to overcrowding in execrable housing and to the collapse of the agrarian economy in Peru, civil war, and massive urban migration. Addressing the "causes of the causes"—a phrase public health experts sometimes use in writing about the social determinants of health and ill-ness—was far beyond the scope of any one nongovernmental organization.[26]

Many of us who were not sick, but caring for these patients in one way or another (whether as physician, nurse, commu-nity health worker, epidemiologist, or administrator), felt over-whelmed and burdened. The closer we were to the suffering, the more overwhelmed and burdened we felt, knowing, as Thomas Merton has said, that "we're a body of broken bones." Even in the midst of this suffering, most of us knew that without a change in policy—without a conversion of it—effective care could not be delivered to the thousands or tens of thousands who needed it. Only a change in policy that led to the public subvention of the diagnosis and effective care of this and other complex diseases could respond to *true* demand, a product of burden of disease rather than the ability to pay for services and goods. Nor could we hope to see the prices of the drugs and diagnostics drop if there were no perceived market, public or private.

"My Mother Is Not a Shirt"
(The Commodification of Care)

Humane and equitable policies could, we knew, save a lot of lives, improve health and well-being, and prevent not only adverse health events but also the economic impact, at the fam-ily and societal level, of disease and disability. These were times that called for both conversion (the processual kind) and com-mitment. But who had the time and resources to respond in an effective manner? Looking back, it is evident that although Pe-ruvian health authorities did not have the requisite resources on hand, at least the need for such changes was becoming clearer in settings such as Lima, a cosmopolitan city in which poverty and disease could not be so readily hidden away.

Returning to liberation theology, it was also easier to see the value of a preferential option for the poor in health care in the hometown of Gustavo Gutiérrez. These were the years, the mid-1990s, when we were lucky enough to meet Father Gustavo and to learn a bit about how he expressed his own pastoral commitments (as distinct from scholarly ones) to a small parish in the Rimac neighborhood of Lima, more established than the shantytowns to the north where we worked, but still populated largely by poor families. Reading his published work in between sessions with desperately ill patients, most of whom survived but all of whom were sick because they were poor and (like the Haitians) thoroughly aware of this noxious synergy, we understood more readily how poverty and privation constituted what the liberation theologians termed "structural sin," the chief barrier, in Peru as in Haiti, to human flourishing.

Some of these barriers were, as noted, constituted by the commodification of health care and others by a failure to invest resources (money, personnel, infrastructure) in the public sector. Many other social determinants of disease related to economic forces beyond the control of the health care system and those who staffed it. But this unacknowledged epidemic of drug-resistant tuberculosis focused us on our mission of providing a preferential option for the poor in health *care*. We worked in a makeshift clinic, took meals together, and held some of our larger meetings in a conference center named (what else?) the Oscar Romero Center.

One of the first conferences we held in the Romero Center was called, grandly enough but earnestly, "The New World Order and the Health of the Poor." Jim Kim was there, as were Ophelia Dahl (another founder of Partners In Health) and Jaime Bayona; Father Roussin had just died, and we were there to honor his memory by advancing the health and social-justice agenda. But how would this come to pass without a deeper understanding of the causes of ill health and of the policies and practices that might prevent it? We were asking these questions—we always asked questions—from the first days of our engagement, and knew even then that we would need to learn more about economics, about cost and effectiveness as understood by those who set policies.

As convinced as we were of the need for conversion among the powerful, we also acknowledged that our own grasp of these matters, including economic ideologies such as those we glossed under the term "neoliberalism," was weak. The Oscar Romero Center symposium was one of those attempts to better understand neo-liberalism (rather than to simply parrot the word). A development economist recommended to us by Gutiérrez, Javier-Maria Iguiñez, was one of the conference presenters; he expressed his concern about the overzealous commodification of basic social services as poetically as any economist we'd met. Although I've tried, in this telling, to interrogate the "sudden epiphany" approach to understanding conversion, I remember very well the claim made that afternoon by Iguiñez. My Spanish was poor at the time, and so I leaned over to ask Dr. Bayona for a clarification. "Did he just say," I whispered, "'my mother is not a shirt'?"

He had.

The crowd, many of them from the neighborhood around Oscar Romero Center and some of them tuberculosis patients, nodded as if this were an important, if obvious, point of departure in any discussion of the economic and social policies affecting the poor. Whether you call our dawning awareness an epiphany or a conversion, we sensed (in spite of anxiety and friction and churn) that we were on the right track. The northern reaches of Lima, the Oscar Romero Center, the fragile houses and sick patients within them, seemed, just then, like important stops along a collective journey toward a preferential option for the poor in health care.

Global Health Equity as the "House of Yes"

"A conversion," writes Gutiérrez, "is the starting point of every spiritual journey."[27] This trajectory, for those seeking to improve the health of those left behind by progress, is usually a long and often painful process: the struggle is not only against disease, our agreed-upon focus, but also against the social conditions that foster it. We engaged in difficult and sometimes circular debates about what the most important milestones on that journey might be, and on which path to take. Although I'm not arguing that *Wells* (or any other work of theology) offers a clear road map for health workers wishing to take on the hardest tasks ranged before medicine and public health, it did offer insights and consolation. Liberation theology offered one interpretive key to understanding structural violence; it complemented frameworks that one might encounter in medicine (the epidemiology of health disparities, say) or in medical anthropology (a field in which many explore how large-scale social forces, from poverty to racism to the collapse of rural economies or "traditional" societies, are *embodied* as pathology and as social suffering).

Other echoes resonated for many among us. We agreed that a spiritual journey that didn't include others, especially the poor, probably isn't one worth taking. Breaking with structural sin required engagement both personal (but "not limited to interior life," as Gutiérrez warned) and social (attacking poverty and structural violence). The old call to material austerity—"Sell all that you have," as in Luke—which some found moving and others less so, served at least as a reminder of one goal of equity. Luke's notion of austerity was never confused, in the poorer neighborhoods of Lima any more than it was in rural Haiti, with the neoliberal dogma then sweeping through the capital cities of Latin America. Many noted that it was not us, but rather our patients and their families, who were selling all they had to find a cure.

The imperative to put the poor first was sometimes a hard sell among medical professionals and other colleagues. But it's possible to exaggerate the amount of resistance that came from doctors or nurses or other frontline providers in Latin America. Their clinical services were often, and sometimes over their objections, sold as commodities, just as laboratory examinations and medications were. Many of them already wished to do more for, and better by, their poorer patients. After all, their mothers weren't shirts either. Those providers who wanted to work "in solidarity" with the destitute sick didn't have a systematic way of doing so; the social safety nets, in most of these settings, were absent or weak, and to be poor and sick meant banging on the doors of a veritable "house of no." We would register this same pattern in Haiti, Peru, Guatemala, and southern Mexico: those who wanted to serve the destitute sick didn't have a robust health system in which to do so.

It doesn't have to be that way. Gutiérrez observed in *Wells* that "the upshot of the option for the poor and their liberation is that in contemporary Latin America we are in a period characterized by a great effort at solidarity."[28] We certainly hoped so. If such solidarity was palpable in medicine and nursing, perhaps especially among younger practitioners, it was slower to penetrate the international health policy circles then governed, sternly whenever resources were deemed scarce in addressing the health problems of the poorest, by an early version of cost-effectiveness analysis not yet attuned to the interrogation of confident claims about both cost and effectiveness. Thus did international health become "the house of no."

Any journey linking social justice to spirituality needs a destination: a world in which there is less violence in whatever form. The journey needs to lead away from structural violence, which is why we were seeking to link the notion of solidarity with that of effectiveness (which we termed, perhaps unoriginally, "pragmatic solidarity"). Effective care for all, "the house of yes," was the utopian destination. This was a lesson we drew from medicine, with its growing focus on good clinical outcomes, but also from *Wells* and other fonts of inspiration. For Gutiérrez also refers explicitly and often to effectiveness. Tellingly, he puts no price tag on it, not because understanding cost is unimportant but rather because it is too important to leave solely to the adjudication of accountants, development economists, or other experts on finance. Such expertise is necessary but insufficient; it too often blocks access to the "house of yes."

Overweening confidence about cost made little sense as regards either prevention or care, and less and less sense during decades in which medicine and public health became more effective for some and less so for others. Consider again pandemic disease at the close of the twentieth century. To believe that we understood how to "cost" (the new verb) health care without understanding the cost (economic and social) of health disparities made little sense in a world still facing premodern threats such as cholera, a disease that had disappeared from places with modern sanitation. During these very years, new cholera vaccines were developed; effective therapy for cholera, when promptly delivered, could prevent almost all deaths; modern sanitation made epidemic transmission unlikely.

It was a similar story in contemplating tuberculosis mortality. Could risk of dying from the disease be uncoupled from risk of acquiring it? New diagnostics and medications, some of them based on an emerging understanding of the changing genetic structure of the pathogen, were altering the course of drug-resistant tuberculosis in the wealthier settings in which the disease, whether drug-susceptible or drug-resistant, was increasingly rare. But these tools were absent from the setting in which tuberculosis took most lives.

These observations do not mean to suggest that we were attempting to attack cost–effectiveness analysis, as applied to these epidemics in Peru or to any other (the growing scourge of AIDS in Africa, for example).[29] But the notion of effectiveness, like cost, needed to be linked to reflection and to the struggle inherent in serving the poorest. This was the linchpin of the matter.

The worship of effectiveness without consideration of equity contains its own traps, as does the fetishization of cost. The most common traps, we learned in confronting all of the illnesses endured by our patients (not only cholera and tuberculosis, but AIDS, many cancers, surgical disease, mental illness), include one constituted by confident claims that *treatment* for these maladies could be given short shrift or ignored among the poor, as long as *prevention* was assured. The treatment-versus-prevention debate is one of the great false dichotomies of modern public health. To do "the most good for the most people" does not inevitably require setting one's sights lower, but this logic led too often to the conclusion that scarce resources needed to be dedicated to culling low-hanging fruit such as vaccine-preventable illness. Better not to look at AIDS or cancer or complex afflictions that were too expensive to prevent, cure, or palliate. Many of these claims about difficult-to-treat illnesses, from AIDS to leukemia, were shown to be empirically false. In any case, these afflictions are not about to go away. The cost of inaction or even ill-informed or overly timid action is still unknown. And yet these confident and unambitious claims underpinned the regnant, if sometimes unspoken, ideologies of international health in the last decades of the twentieth century and in the first decade of this one. Thus does international health, given a welcome shift toward global health equity, remain stuck in "the house of no."

Health Systems, Justice, Compassion

Saying *yes* to these patients and their families sometimes brought us in conflict with those charged with saying yes or no to health services for the poorest. A shrinkage of the social compact in Latin America, of the sort termed "structural adjustment," led to even sharper conflict about health policies and public expenditures. Since our skills and motivation had more to do with delivering services than winning arguments, we did not relish this conflict, even though we knew that it was inescapable. Early on, we engaged in dispiriting debates about whether or not it was "possible" or "wise" to treat patients with highly drug-resistant tuberculosis. On one such occasion, I gave a presentation about working with community health workers to improve the outcomes of tuberculosis treatment in rural Haiti, and then added a defense of expanding care options for patients sick from drug-resistant strains. This would necessarily require investments in laboratories and in the so-called second-line drugs, as had been the case in New York and elsewhere. Since these had already been documented in Lima, such investments were urgently needed in Peru. The director of the national tuberculosis program took a sharply divergent view. Treatment of such cases did not feature in national guidelines and are not a priority, he said. His parting shot has always stuck with me: "If you really wish to make a preferential option for the poor, you should spend your resources on building health systems like the national tuberculosis program."

He was right at least as far as building national systems are concerned; we just wanted to build a better, more responsive one. Nongovernmental organizations are often slow to learn this lesson, which is one of the chief reasons, too rarely acknowledged, that so much conflict occurs between NGOs and governments. Building health systems was part of building social safely nets, yet another form of social conversion required to attack poverty meaningfully. But such utopian and unrealized visions did nothing for those already sick with drug-resistant tuberculosis; nor did they make poor people with AIDS or cancer or schizophrenia or epilepsy any more visible in arid and often circular international health debates. Health systems needed to be built to respond effectively to the ranking health problems of "the people" (to use the local term, widespread in Latin America and found in Gutiérrez's work) and to ensure equity of access for neglected problems afflicting the poor. To anthropomorphize, health systems need to be just and effective; they could even be compassionate and merciful, even though they seldom are.[30]

Such public-health debates were bound to be wrenching. They can become more lucid and informed by infusions of resources and knowledge and new technologies. They are usually arid and circular when ideological and sharply conflictual when constrained by perceived and real scarcity, or by violence.

Social justice work can hardly avoid conflict, especially when we attend to both the suffering of the poor as a "people" who sometimes identify with each other, and to individual patients burdened by serious illness and also by poverty. Liberation theology expects and confronts conflict, since it is generated in part, by reflection on structural violence: "Gutiérrez became a theologian and a priest because he believed evangelization is a more

powerful response to poverty than violence, and his main concern is precisely how to be Christian in the context of global
poverty."[31] Evangelization is not a familiar term in medicine or
public health, and still less so in anthropology, but using it metaphorically meant spreading the good news about new tools (preventives, diagnostics, therapeutics) that could save lives and palliate suffering. New tools require new resources for deployment,
which in the case of Peruvian MDRTB were absent; hence the
conflict.

It had been the same story in rural Haiti—lots of illness, no
modern medical care—and now we saw health disparities in a
bustling city at the close of a civil conflict. The story would recur, with local variation, whenever basic services for the poorest
were delivered poorly or not at all, which is to say pretty much
everywhere. Hence the recurrence of the conflict regardless of
the personalities and demeanors of those engaged in this struggle.

Gutiérrez had his own difficulties with the local Catholic hierarchy, we knew, but it didn't occur to us just then that we might
be in a position to mediate him to a non-Catholic, much less a
medical, audience. "Mediate" means something specific, of course:
it's not to dilute but rather to translate, and he hardly needed translation in his native country and continent. As physicians, nurses,
and community health workers, we were careful not to confuse
our work with that of those struggling, through nonviolent means,
to liberate themselves from poverty. But we did see ourselves as
part of the effort, in Haiti and Peru and elsewhere, to free those
we served from suffering and early deaths from preventable and
treatable diseases. The more scientific progress achieves, the more
scandalous it is that people are excluded from its benefits. Like the
poor, we were caught in a struggle: a struggle for resources (clinics,
laboratories, hospitals, medications, personnel, training) and against
policies and perceptions that held some illnesses to be untreatable
when they occur among the poor.

Experience, first in Haiti and then in Peru, taught us that in
order to be effective we needed to be part of a larger effort to
build health systems, and that effort itself is part of a still larger

effort to increase social protection, ultimately contributing to the grand vision of a world without poverty. There was nothing new about this vision in a dystopian present. Critics, local and homegrown, called on us to show that such interventions might make a difference to overall trends in the "burden of disease on a population level." This is public-health-speak rather than God-talk. Like God-talk, public-health-speak not only has its own jargon and generative paradigms, but also its importance and its irrefutable utility. Who among us did not wish to make a difference?

Although our own wish to make a difference was rarely a primary concern of our patients or their loved ones, we agreed that too much of the discussion was based on ideology rather than empirical evidence. Hard evidence may rarely inform either theology or philosophy, but there were echoes of this call for empirical analysis within liberationist circles, too. This is one of the reasons that Gutiérrez cites not only scripture, but also research from many fields; it's why he often cites Oscar Romero, whose embrace of liberation theology was informed by a deepening knowledge of structural violence: "Why do the rural poor become part of society only in the coffee- and cotton-picking seasons?"[32] Gutiérrez adds: "The will to conversion should lead to this kind of concrete analysis."

The same sort of analysis ("concrete," in Gutiérrez's term, and attuned to social change) must necessarily inform a preferential option for the poor in health care, since the meaning of such a preference changes as rapidly as do social conditions and epidemiology. Looking at the global burden of disease, and at gaps in delivery, we saw and read of millions of avoidable deaths. These are the "topographies of vast pain" of which theologian Kathleen O'Connor writes in *Lamentations and the Tears of the World*: close to ten million children and young adults, almost all of them poor, died in the 1990s from malaria, tuberculosis, AIDS, complications of childbirth, pneumonia, trauma, and cancers for which therapy had been shown to be effective. It was no wonder that public health authorities, starved for resources, carved up their pittance sparingly.

Because a preferential option for the poor in health care, derived in part from liberation theology, was utopian and aspirational, and because it could, we believed, address much needless suffering, we set out to convince (convert) friends and colleagues outside of conventional public health circles. Some of them also found liberation theology inspiring or instructive. We were not trying to convert them in the sense of religious conversion; there are many deep wells from which to drink, and metanoia occurs in often mysterious ways. We were seeking, rather, to argue a pragmatic point, that the effective *delivery* of health care to the poor could and should save millions of lives.

The true effectiveness of modern medicine and public health had never been assessed, even by the 1990s, in the very settings in which they were likely to bring about the greatest declines in premature death and suffering because they had never, or rarely, been funneled through a system able to deliver such services. There were at least three sides to our case. One, the denial of adequate services needed to be remedied; two, remedying this inequality would bring about the results we expected in terms of improved health outcomes; three, addressing health disparities would have returns well beyond the expected ones, as do other efforts to promote social justice. We were convinced of this more than a decade earlier in Haiti, and would later see it proved in Rwanda. As the list of treatable afflictions grows, because new discoveries render the untreatable ones treatable, our aspirations must keep pace. Moving these aspirations forward among those charged with addressing these afflictions among the poor is so hard that it requires something tantamount to conversion, among our ranks and others, and a deep well of resources to sustain progress.

"Concrete analysis" of poverty reduction reveals enormous changes over the past decade. Using a framework like the Millennium Development Goals, which is not a prescriptive theoretical plan but rather a set of objectives or goals against which progress might be measured, suggests a worldwide improvement in health outcomes.[33] But the improvement has been unevenly distributed. In sub-Saharan Africa, only Rwanda (on which more below) is poised to meet all of the health-related goals and most of the others. Russia and most of its satellites saw a collapse of health systems and social safety nets as the Soviet Union became the Former Soviet Union. Staying with the topic of drug-resistant tuberculosis, Russia alone has tens of thousands of cases; the tuberculosis epidemic there was amplified by an epidemic of incarceration not dissimilar from that registered in the United States. But unlike the New York outbreak, which also started in prisons and homeless shelters, the Russian authorities did not (and at the time could not) invest heavily in a public-sector response, and drug-resistant tuberculosis was, again, allowed to spread, becoming a leading cause of death among detainees young and old. This is what led us from Peru to Siberia, where we again learned that effective care for this disease could bring mortality rates within prisons almost to zero.[34]

So why, with uneven progress and growing inequality, can poverty reduction be held to be to on track? Much of the aggregate global improvement has occurred because a single country, China, can claim to have lifted between 400 and 600 million people out of poverty in the past couple of decades.[35]

But, there too, economic growth doesn't solve all problems. Concrete analysis of social changes would note the connection between rapid urbanization and economic growth, but also the collapse of rural health services.[36] The persistence of drug-resistant tuberculosis and other chronic infections, including AIDS and hepatitis C, can be observed in China and in other rapidly expanding economies. The rise of new noncommunicable pathologies, from diabetes to major mental illnesses, is widely reported in many settings of rapid industrialization.

From Haiti to Rwanda and Back Again

The preferential option for the poor made by pathogens and pathogenic forces, both social and microbial, is rendered in sharp relief in times of social upheaval. A familiar trajectory in my work, and in that of Partners In Health, leads from Haiti to

Rwanda, the country wracked by the greatest spasm of violence ever to afflict that continent. But the power of an "equity response" (a preferential option for the poor in health care and related social services) to counter these pathogens can also be revealed, as the experience of Rwanda suggests.

Nineteen years ago this week, a systematic and state-sponsored killing spree, targeting the Tutsi minority and those deemed sympathetic to their plight, began during Holy Week. Within a few months, up to a million people were murdered. There were discrepant claims of causality, of course, and transnational complicity, and the host of sorry excuses and self-exculpatory declarations always heard regarding genocide and war. Debates about these events continue, as do their violent echoes in the Congo and elsewhere. I will not review them here, in a conversation about a preferential option for the poor in health care and in an essay about conversion and solidarity. Here I will say instead that, although Easter in Rwanda is always a time of mourning, it is nonetheless now true that Rwanda's rebirth offers a contrapuntal message more fit for Easter.

Contemplating this rebirth offers lessons for anyone interested in public health and in well-being, just as it does for those interested in seeking to understand how best to promote recovery after a social cataclysm. At the close of 1994, Rwanda lay in ruins. Many of its hospitals and clinics had been damaged or destroyed; others were simply abandoned; a large portion of health workers had been killed or were in refugee camps. These settlements were thinned by cholera and other "camp epidemics" and by a rising tide of AIDS, tuberculosis, and malaria. Child mortality was the highest in the world; malnutrition was rampant. Many development experts were ready to write the small nation off as a lost cause, a failed state, a hopeless enterprise.

Today, as noted, Rwanda is the only country in sub-Saharan Africa on track to meet each of the health-related Millennium Development Goals by 2015. More than 93 percent of Rwandan infants are inoculated against eleven vaccine-preventable illnesses, up from 25 percent against five diseases in the year after the genocide. Over the past decade, death during childbirth has declined by more than 60 percent. Rwanda is one of only two countries on the continent to achieve the goal of universal access to AIDS therapy.

Deaths attributed to AIDS, tuberculosis, and malaria have dropped even more steeply in Rwanda, as have deaths registered among children under five. There's still a long way to go, but these are some of the steepest declines in mortality ever documented, anywhere and at any time, as we have concluded in reviewing these data.[37] This is surely a striking example of social transformation, a sharp turn away from structural violence.

What accounts for this turnaround, this systemic conversion? Claims of causality in recovery are also disputed, but we believe that these successes are the result of health authorities' pursuit of a proper health system, one prioritizing the needs of the poorest and most vulnerable. It's due in part to a health system, over a decade in the making, which reaches out to the rural poor (greater than 80 percent of Rwandans live in rural areas) and includes a community-based health insurance scheme. In other words, a system able to make, or at least begin to make, a preferential option for the poor in health and social protection.

Private-sector partners, from churches and nongovernmental organizations and donors, are exhorted by the Rwandan health authorities to participate in building the same health system rather than parallel ones; thus do they add up to more than the sum of their parts and also serve as an object lesson in pragmatic solidarity. For example, Rwanda still faces a great shortage of skilled health providers but is addressing it through innovative delivery models of community-based care, nurse-run clinics, and district hospitals. As deaths in childbirth and those due to vaccine-preventable illness, AIDS, malaria, and tuberculosis decline, more energy and resources are invested in responding to other chronic diseases, including diabetes and mental illness and other complex afflictions. Until this year, Rwanda had zero oncologists (but plenty of cancer) and only one pediatric cardiologist working in the public sector (but plenty of children in need of cardiac care). Last year, with faculty from a dozen US medical centers, Rwanda embarked on a seven-year initiative to train physicians and nurses in these and other specialties deemed a priority. Rwandan public-sector institutions are thus strengthened, even as medical education builds local capacity for the long term.

Haiti is struggling to get on the same path. The earthquake that on January 12, 2010, killed and maimed perhaps a quarter of a million also leveled most of Haiti's government infrastructure. It occasioned not only a torrent of informal theodicy but also an outpouring of international solidarity. But both the event and the response were humbling reminders that equitable and effective health services cannot be easily delivered without infrastructure. This challenge of effective delivery is especially humbling in public health, since long experience suggests that strong public institutions are a prerequisite of meaningful gains in these areas. Those who work with nongovernmental organizations and universities and churches are by definition outside of these public institutions. Some have defined themselves in opposition to a state deemed inept or inefficient, at best, or corrupt and violent, at worst. But how will those living in poverty hope to have basic social and economic rights—what some liberation theologians have termed the right to survive—if more is not invested in making such institutions work? If no effort is made to transform (convert) them?

Consider, one last time, the cholera epidemic that followed the quake. The first Haitian likely fell ill on October 12, 2010, when a homeless and mentally ill man from Mirebalais, suffered an abrupt onset of profuse, watery diarrhea. He died within hours. Then two of the mortuary assistants who had prepared his body for burial fell ill; less than two weeks after the first care, there were scores of cases of profuse diarrhea in Mirebalais and in the villages connected to it by tributaries of the small river snaking through the town—a source of drinking water for the first victim, but also for many others. The epidemic then raced west along Haiti's largest river, reaching the coastal cities of Gonaïves and St. Marc a week later. On October 22 health authorities officially announced that cholera had reached Haiti. At this writing, less than three years later, the Haitian epidemic is far and away the largest in the world: there have been more than 650,000 cases, with 8,053 deaths.[38]

As with all lethal epidemics, immodest claims of causality, homegrown and international, ensued.[39] Haiti's cholera epidemic was not, as was commonly assumed by experts on "natural" disasters, the result of the earthquake that had occurred nine months previously. Indeed, there were proportionally fewer cases in the urban quake zone and in camps full of "internally displaced persons." As in Rwanda in 1995, the Haiti cholera epidemic started and spread as a result of the social upheaval that followed the fall of the dictatorship and two military coups d'états, events clearly the result of human agency, and of a stunning lack of public investment in modern sanitation, of similar social origin. The introduction of a new pathogen was because the latter of these two coups was followed, in 2004, by the arrival of peacekeeping forces from cholera-endemic areas. The epidemic likely began after a troop rotation in 2010, but would have followed a similar course if introduced several years earlier.

The pathogen, once introduced by poor or absent sanitation to rural Haiti's streams and rivers, spread rapidly along long-standing local fault lines. These include not only a lack of sanitation and safe drinking water but also a lack of access to health care for the mentally ill, as the case of the young man from Mirebalais reminds us, and for the rural and urban poor in general. In reporting this first case, two of my closest colleagues, Drs. Louise Ivers and David Walton, made the following observation:

> This patient's case illustrates the relationship between an infectious disease epidemic, mental health, and globalization. It highlights the fact that to provide and maintain

health in circumstances of destitute poverty where many factors are at play, addressing no one single factor will result in success and that mental health is a critical component. . . . Attempts to address individual pieces of health without consideration of the whole are as the Haitian proverb goes, "like washing your hands and drying them in the dirt."[40]

This is how structural violence gets in the body as cholera. How do we get it out? By considering the whole, as my colleagues note, and by building just and effective and compassionate systems to protect the vulnerable, as the Rwandans now seek to do. The first step is to tend to those already sick, since no one should die from cholera, and indeed mortality dropped to zero in settings where effective diagnosis and care became readily available. There are also, as mentioned, new vaccines that could offer some protection to the most vulnerable. But we all know that clean water and modern sanitation are the most reliable and enduring ways to prevent the spread of waterborne disease.[41] The previous cholera epidemic in Latin America afforded many in Peru (and elsewhere) to advance the cause of modern sanitation and safe drinking water as a public good, even as community organizations worked to prevent and treat cholera and other waterborne illness in their neighborhoods. The current Latin American cholera epidemic, which started in Haiti, offers the same chance of fighting for the same basic services there.[42] This cannot be done, we have argued, without moving from the notion of "aid" to that of accompaniment. It cannot be done without contributing to stronger public health systems. It cannot be done without sustained engagement between all partners who wish to add up to more than the sum of their parts.

It cannot be done, in other words, without changing the policies governing much, perhaps most, development assistance and humanitarian aid. Everyone who engages in the process of hastening progress, whether couched in the language of the development enterprise or in social-justice terms, and of making sure that fewer people need the charity and mercy of others simply to survive, will encounter certain tasks outside of their comfort zones (to use an Americanism). For me, this familiar and comfortable place was within clinics and hospitals and classrooms, and within the local moral worlds of our patients. Stepping out of it involved, as my friends and colleagues Jaime Bayona and Jim Kim observed twenty years ago, seeking to change *policy* where it was made.

In considering the health problems of the poor, the importance of the social determinants of them, from working conditions to housing and clean water, is obvious. It is not that physicians or other providers of care are called to know about all of these complex matters before commenting on policies or programs. The point is rather to remember that some of our fellows are more vulnerable than others to pathogens and pathogenic forces that can be studied and known, as can the construction of vulnerability itself. Those most affected by pathogens always have something to add to this knowledge, but it is rarely they who are the architects of their great vulnerability. Changing policies and paradigms within those institutions, whether in Port-au-Prince or Kigali or Washington or New York or Geneva or Rome, is a part of accompaniment and also part of the conversion required for a more solidarity-based approach to human progress.

Accompaniment, Propinquity, and Systemic Change

To accompany someone is, as noted elsewhere in this book, to go somewhere with him or her, to break bread together, to be present on a journey with a beginning and an end. The process is humbling, since there is always an element of temporal and experiential mystery, of openness, in accompaniment. Grand theories and well-laid plans often come to naught; clear objectives and "deliverables" and metrics are all too rare in such endeavors.

Even good intentions and long experience sometimes fail us. Accompaniment with discernment also requires asking tough questions: Are we doing the right thing? Have we carried through? Have we followed up? Do we understand as fully as we might? Are we doing enough? Is the problem solved? If an effort is not laden with anxiety, it's probably not accompaniment, or it's just the beginning of the effort.

The process of discernment is rarely straightforward, because listening carefully is hard to do. Listening with "reverent attention" (to use Kathleen O'Connor's phrase) is even harder, especially when the subject at hand is social suffering. Soliciting such judgments from those accompanied can be uplifting or painful, surprising or mundane, obvious or difficult to decipher. But in most cases, it requires social proximity or, at the very least, reliable interlocutors. In his book about a theology of accompaniment, Roberto Goizueta of Boston College writes the following: "To 'opt for the poor' is thus to place ourselves *there*, to *accompany* the poor person in his or her life, death, and struggle for survival."[43] Goizueta, who draws heavily on the work of Gutiérrez, is focused on the accompaniment of Latinos in the United States, especially recent immigrants facing relative poverty, poor labor conditions, and (often enough) precarious legal status. Physical and social proximity is important to accompaniment, but uncommon in a country segregated by race or class or both:

> As a society, we are happy to help and serve the poor, as long as we don't have to walk *with* them where they walk, that is, as long as we can minister to them from our safe enclosures. The poor can then remain passive objects of our actions, rather than friends, *compañeros* and *compañeras* with whom we interact. As long as we can be sure that we will not have to live with them, and thus have interpersonal relationships with them, we will try to help "the poor"—but, again, only from a controllable, geographical distance.[44]

Propinquity is part of the spirituality of accompaniment. It's not always the easy part, especially for those who understand that the world is one, as opposed to divided into First, Second, and Third worlds. If, as Father Jim Keenan has observed, true hospitality requires "entering into the chaos of another's life," we can expect that walking with those whose lives are rendered chaotic by poverty will not be easy or conflict free. Nor is accompaniment really possible, of course, when erstwhile *accompagnateurs* are cloistered in monasteries or sequestered in ivory towers, although these are known to be good places in which to write and reflect. Doctors and nurses and other healers know this, too. None of the new information technologies and diagnostic tools can replace the need to examine and speak with a patient.

If accompaniment of the sick is more often about walking together in companionable silence than about prophetic denunciation, it is nonetheless true that dramatic circumstance often requires deploring the "event" violence that structural violence generates and invariably worsens. This is not to argue that violence, structured or otherwise, is our inevitable lot as a species, even though it is hard, for those caught up in privation and war, to imagine a world free of it.

As both preacher and writer, Gutiérrez is of course an inveterate citer of scripture. But since his way of doing theology rehabilitates social analysis, including the historical study of structural violence against the poor of certain times and places, he also cites his contemporaries, especially those struggling against violent authoritarian regimes and violent economic conditions. One leading contemporary source—a bishop who was converted, in the eyes of some, by paying greater attention to violence affecting the poor—was of course Oscar Romero.

Gutiérrez has been a faithful friend and echo of Romero. He returns often to the archbishop's words, and to his understandings, for many reasons. The two are comparable in certain ways. They were born around the same time and came of age as priests in the same era; both regarded themselves as part of the same "people," even though historians and demographers and political scientists (to say nothing of anthropologists) would note that El Salvador and Peru were and are worlds apart. One became a bishop while the other became a theologian, yet both helped build the progressive wing of the Latin American church. They did this not only by seeking to accompany members of parishes in San Salvador and Lima. They saw their work, from early in their vocations, as including what those outside of the church might well call "policy work." How else would they both end up in places such as Rome during the Second Vatican Council or the conferences held in Puebla or Medellín?

They were also committed to learning. Concrete analysis of structural violence is never easy, in part because human suffering linked to injustice invariably generates, as noted, discrepant claims of causality. Romero's own understandings of causality changed over time, representing a kind of conversion informed by empirical research, though that's not the term anyone in El Salvador would likely use to describe the testimonies and analyses of event and structural violence there. When Romero's process of discernment, informed by theologians but even more so by the suffering of the Salvadoran poor, led him to denounce both event violence (the civil war and the arms that fueled it) and structural violence, he paid, in 1980, the price that many others have paid.

Romero's martyrdom was a turning point for his country and his church (professing Catholics, clergy and religious, the hierarchy), as it was for many of us seeking to understand how violence and conflict in Latin America might be connected to people and countries shielded from that violence. (The conflict in El Salvador was exacerbated, as Romero insisted, by US foreign policy.) The El Salvador civil war was also an inflection point, for all of those seeking to provide medical care and other social services to the region's poorest. From El Salvador to Guatemala and Nicaragua and Honduras, similar conflicts erupted, with similar effects on the delivery of health care.[45] Thus was poor health care both cause and consequence of conflict.

Six years after Romero's death, the fall of the Duvalier dictatorship opened the way to a violent sequence of military-dominated Haitian governments, also supported by some US administrations, leading some astute observers to speak of the "Salvadorization" of Haiti. But such conditions obtain across space and time, as noted at the outset of this essay; the government of France played a similar, corrosive role in Rwanda prior to and just after the genocide there. Doing one's homework about structural violence would mean one thing in Haiti, another in El Salvador, and still another in Russia or Rwanda, but it always means trying to learn how poverty and inequality come to be and how they persist and change over time. It means waking up to what seem like impersonal forces beyond human control but which are, rather, social suffering. Systemic change for the better will not come about without it.

None of us wishes to live in violent or disrupted places. But as we live in one world, not three, we need to move beyond that aphorism, "think globally, act locally." It is always the time of cholera somewhere in our world.

Conversion, Solidarity, and the Fight against Structural Violence

Recent events in Haiti and Rwanda remind us that the problems to which liberation theology is a response are alive and well, even though many of us believe, to paraphrase Martin Luther King Jr., that the arc of history bends toward justice. Not long after the Second World War, Bertrand Russell argued that "the secret of happiness is to face the fact that the world is horrible, horrible, horrible."[46] Then as now it is important to add, as liberation theologians and doctors do, that it is much more horrible for some than others. Rather than indulge, here, in a discussion of relative and absolute poverty, or the merits of intervening in one place versus another (as we are all forced to do, every day), or of varied and changing notions of triage, I will close with a simple assertion. The indignities of poverty and inequality are bad; to be poor and sick, even worse; and to be sick and poor and a victim of violence in the absence of a compassionate and just health system is to be subjected to something horrible, horrible, horrible.

Confronting this synergy of plagues, whether in Rwanda wracked by genocide or Europe wracked by war, requires discernment and, at times, resistance. But resistance to what, precisely? Resistance to structural sin, certainly, and to the lure of violence in all its forms. But another commonly confronted sin may be the sin of pride, which, among us who are relatively capable, well-off, and powerful, is linked often to a quest not for power in the crass sense but for personal efficacy. This is the flip side of the humiliation of poverty and the resentment and indignation born of it. Not all progressives blessed with Father Gustavo's scholarly gifts are also humble and kind, as Dan Groody, writing of others ostensibly laboring in the same vineyard, reports: "Beneath the theological words and the social analysis were attitudes of self-righteousness, judgmentalism, and aggressiveness that left me wanting to fight for liberation from a deeper place."[47]

That deeper place was, for me, the world of the sick and also those who care for them, from community health workers to nurses and physicians. I have found, in hospitals and clinics around the world, a bit less self-righteousness and aggressiveness than is seen among those charged (usually by ourselves) with attacking structural violence and promoting human rights, or with writing about such matters. This is in part because of the humbling nature of caring for the sick, whether in Harvard teaching hospitals or squatter settlements or within prison walls, even though far too little time is spent with patients and their families and even though clinicians tend to know little about how poverty gets embodied.[48] The proximity to suffering is humbling, especially when a clinician takes responsibility for easing it. A focus on "good outcomes" (though not without risk) requires, especially in such settings and especially regarding patients with chronic and difficult-to-treat illness, as much a commitment to accompaniment as to understanding medical progress. Just as a preferential option for the poor is not about winning an argument, neither is the effective and compassionate practice of clinical medicine in settings of poverty about the cheap showmanship of diagnosis without delivery of care.

I will conclude by returning to the daunting word "conversion," which I've insistently linked to process and to ostensibly anodyne terms such as social change. These are linked in important, indeed causal, ways. Attacking poverty requires the conversion of people and the institutions they create and shape. As in the struggle against slavery, crass poverty and the social suffering associated with it and all forms of exclusion must become increasingly regarded as intolerable, regardless of where on the globe destitution and misery persist. The way forward will not likely come from prescriptive master paradigms or from the arrogantly totalizing frameworks that emerged in Europe during the tumultuous nineteenth century. These have served us poorly, as we learned in the following century, the one in which most of us were born and came of age, converted from children to adults.

Many paths seek to rehabilitate the universal quest for human development even as we acknowledge that the paths, perhaps already laid before us, are not well blazed. We don't often know the best ways forward, for ourselves or anyone else, and so need to incorporate some sort of humility into the journey, which proceeds necessarily in fellowship. One of the struggles incumbent on all of us is to resist confident and contradictory claims made for both causality and action in the struggle against poverty. Development economics is full of these, but faddishness, self-righteousness, and ready judgment of others are no strangers to other forms of social justice work, either. It is surely true that economic growth with equity, and in a way that does not destroy the planet we live on, is required for next steps in poverty reduction. But just as it is true that human beings are not exchangeable commodities, so too must we acknowledge that even equitable economic growth is not a panacea for social suffering, nor will it replace compassion and mercy and solidarity as values worth valuing.[49] My mother is not a shirt, nor will she ever be one.

If we cannot sublimate fully our own quest for personal efficacy, what can we do to serve others, and especially the most vulnerable? A preferential option for the poor and accompaniment and structural violence are not the only good ideas out there, but rather remind us of work yet to be done.

Some of that work is analytic. What might we do to better understand poverty as "structured evil," to use an expression that would find favor with the theologians cited here? It is an Enlightenment ideal that greater understanding may lead to informed and reparative action. It's a sound ideal, even if the way forward is rarely clear because there is almost never just one way forward. There are, as Father Gustavo likes to say, *mil maneras*— a thousand ways—to take on contemporary poverty. But some ways are unlikely to advance the cause of social justice. One dead end is the path of cynicism, or claims that any quest for truths regarding poverty, privation, or social suffering are so fraught with moral hazard that it's not worth the effort. Medicine and public health would be stalled by such thinking, as would the scientific and technological progress that promises, if harnessed wisely, to advance the cause of health equity.

Understanding how the suffering of the poorest is perpetuated is not the same as fighting it: the real protagonists of the war on poverty will of course include those struggling to free themselves from it. But if we believe that knowledge can inform practice—if we believe in praxis as pragmatic solidarity—then it is best to have intellectual *and* pragmatic accompaniment as we move the social justice agenda forward.

Gustavo Gutiérrez, by linking discernment to an understanding of the experience of poverty and to the ability to imagine a world without it, offers precisely this form of accompaniment. Latin America is often the "country" to which he refers, and its inhabitants the "people" to whom he refers. On first reading of *Wells*, these uses seem ill-founded, much like the term "Hispanic" in the United States, a term that immodestly hopes to encompass affluent Cuban Americans in Miami and refugees from poor villages in strife-torn El Salvador or Guatemala (a conflation that Roberto Goizueta dissects in his book on accompaniment). On first reading, one wonders (at least this one did) if Gutiérrez uses these terms without full knowledge of changing conceptions of the nation-state, about which political economists, including some deemed subversive in Latin America, have long written. But a slow conversion creeps into a later reading of this and other works, from *A Theology of Liberation* to his book on Job, when it occurs to this reader that the full power, spiritual and analytic, of liberation theology is seen in its acknowledgment of the powerfully constraining force exercised by historically structured and transnational social forces and also the liberating potential of the struggle against poverty and war and premature death—against social suffering and against structural violence.

That's the point of a book on spirituality and social justice: that in times and places where books are usually written and read, it is important that we resist looking away from social suffering and pretending that the world's poorest *do* live in a country of their own, a nation hidden away from view so that its suffering and sickness and strife might not trouble those who live in the country of the healthy and prosperous.

Guided by these notions—an option for the poor and accompaniment and structural violence—one need not ask, "How do we make the journey after conversion?" It's how to make that journey part of the transformative change we will need to end poverty and related pathologies that matters most. Accompanying the destitute sick on a journey away from premature suffering and death—out of the country of social suffering, through the door of yes—is not a single life's work, but rather the work of many, pulling together and over long years and many miles.

Notes

[1] This essay is not intended to be more than that, an essay. I won't seek to review any literature in this overview or to do more than document claims made about the outcomes of various efforts to provide medical care in some of the settings discussed here; most of the non-medical references cited are to anthropologists who have been my teachers and colleagues.

[2] This point was made clear to me in a recent discussion with Jean-Bertrand Aristide, whose personal experience of struggling against poverty in Haiti is discussed below and in his own early works, especially in his collection of sermons from his pastorship of the Church of St. Jean Bosco in Port-au-Prince, *In the Parish of the Poor: Writings from Haiti* (Maryknoll, NY: Orbis Books, 1990), and in *Aristide: An Autobiography* (Maryknoll, NY: Orbis Books, 1993). The more recent chapters of his life, which has included seven years of exile in South Africa, have been written by others (including many with only passing interest in liberation theology), but Aristide continues to read (and, we hope, write) in a tradition that draws not only on theology but on psychology, anthropology, and linguistics.

[3] Amy Wilentz, *The Rainy Season: Haiti since Duvalier* (New York: Simon & Schuster, 1989).

[4] Penny Lernoux, *People of God: The Struggle for World Catholicism* (New York: Penguin Books, 1990).

[5] For further ethnographic reading on the role of the church and "base communities" in the social justice struggles in Latin America throughout the latter part of the twentieth century, see Roger N. Lancaster's *Thanks to God and the Revolution: Popular Religion and Class Consciousness in the New Nicaragua* (New York: Columbia University Press, 1988), or John Burdick's *Looking for God in Brazil: The Progressive Catholic Church in Urban Brazil's Religious Arena* (Berkeley: University of California Press, 1993). In addition, see Amy Wilentz's foreword to *In the Parish of the Poor*, the previously cited collection of some of the sermons of Jean-Bertrand Aristide, who was the leading proponent of both liberation theology in Haiti and of the break from dictatorship.

[6] Amy Wilentz, *Farewell, Fred Voodoo: A Letter from Haiti* (New York: Simon & Schuster, 2013), 32.

[7] The quotation marks are, alas, necessary. A spike in prices of food and other essential commodities was linked to policies made far from Gonaïves or Port-au-Prince or any other Haitian city, which is why protests (some of them violent) against this sharp rise in the cost of surviving occurred in many parts of the world at the time. For a thoughtful review of the large-scale social and economic processes—and policies—underpinning these irruptions (to use Gutiérrez's term) in Haiti and elsewhere, see development sociologists Raj Patel's and Philip McMichael's "A Political Economy of the Food Riot," *Review: A*

Journal of the Fernand Braudel Center 12, no. 1 (2009): 9–35. Such fundamentally resocialized understandings of twentieth-century food insecurity and famine have long been the focus of work by Amartya Sen and others seeking to "explain" and interpret the complex relationship between unequal development, persistent poverty, participatory democracy, and freedom from want. (See also Janam Mukherjee's dissertation, "Hungry Bengal: War, Famine, Riots and the End of Empire, 1939–1946," University of Michigan, 2011.) This quest for an understanding of *causality* is at the heart of most discussions, public and private, about misfortune, just as it is at the heart of this book and of the conversations between all of those who dare to examine suffering and misfortune as something more than an accident of history or, worse, of nature—and thus beyond our control. As Mike Davis notes in *Late Victorian Holocausts* (London: Verso, 2001), such catastrophes occurred in the nineteenth century because of, rather than in spite of, policies set in the heart of colonial empires. They were more a reflection or marker of connections between the rich and poor rather than the lack of connection. The same is true of the famines that occurred in China in the late twentieth century. This transregional (which is usually transnational) view of both misfortune and of poverty is as central to liberation theology, which is reliably catholic (lowercase) in this regard, as it is to political economy or to the *longue durée* school of social history.

⁸ My first published papers in anthropology examined these changing modes of explanation in the context of rapid social change. See, for example, "Bad Blood, Spoiled Milk: Body Fluids as Moral Barometers in Rural Haiti," *American Ethnologist* 15, no. 1 (1988): 62–83; or "Sending Sickness: Sorcery, Politics, and Changing Concepts of AIDS in Rural Haiti," *Medical Anthropologist Quarterly* 4, no. 1 (1990): 6–27.

⁹ This illusion is clear to theologians who attend to pain and suffering. Kathleen O'Connor, in writing about the book of Lamentations, notes that "it evokes readers' worlds in different ways. For survivors of civil wars, destroyed cities, and genocides, for refugees and for those who subsist in famine and destitute poverty, the poetry mirrors reality with frightening exactitude. When, like me, readers live in relative safety and prosperity, Lamentations calls forth loss and pain more narrowly, personally, and indirectly. Yet even in the prosperous United States there are normal human losses to lament, deaths, disappointments, and hidden depression with which to contend. There are broken marriages, catastrophic illnesses, and violence among our children, hatred between groups, and debilitating poverty exacerbated by wealth all around. Behind the wealth and power of the United States hide despair and a violent culture of denial that drains our humanity. For our sake and for the sake of the world over which we try callously to preside, these things demand lamentation." See *Lamentations and the Tears of the World* (Maryknoll, NY: Orbis Books, 2002), 5.

[10] Arthur Kleinman, Veena Das, and Margaret Lock, eds., *Social Suffering* (Berkeley: University of California Press, 1997).

[11] I mention moral philosophers because John Rawls, in his book *A Theory of Justice*, writes little of social justice as the term is used here or in liberation theology. His successors in the field point this out in an edited volume, *The Ethics of Assistance: Morality and the Distant Needy*. Peter Singer recalls that when he first read Rawls's book, he was "astonished that a book of nearly 600 pages with that title could fail to tackle the injustice of unequal wealth between different societies" (Peter Singer, "Outsiders and Our Obligations to Those beyond Our Borders," in *The Ethics of Assistance: Morality and the Distant Needy*, ed. Deen K. Chatterjee [Cambridge: Cambridge University Press, 2004], 11–32). See also the superb essay by Thomas Pogge in the same volume.

[12] Anthropologists often trace modern Haitian ways of explaining misfortune to the slave plantations from which Haiti was born. A wonderful essay about folk healing by Karen McCarthy Brown puts it this way: for the early Haitians, "natural powers such as those of storm, drought, and disease paled before social powers such as those of the slave holder" ("Systematic Remembering, Systematic Forgetting: Ogou in Haiti," in *Africa's Ogun: Old World and New*, ed. Sandra Barnes [Bloomington: Indiana University Press, 1989], 67.) See also her essay, "Afro-Caribbean Spirituality: A Haitian Case Study," *Second Opinion* 11 (July 1989): 36–57.

[13] I'm referring to "old-school" nineteenth-century social theory as it played out in the pages of continental social thought and political philosophy—and in brisk, sometimes deadly, social debate. These discussions would continue in anthropology, sociology, and social theory throughout the twentieth century and beyond. They are all debates about causality, about which I learned plenty from Haitians and also in classes where notions such as the "culture of poverty" and its relationship to social suffering was much discussed, just as etiologies of medical conditions were discussed in my medical training. On the former, see the incisive overview, *Blaming the Victim*, by William Ryan (1971; New York: Vintage Books, 1976). I've also tried to interrogate claims of causality, both immodest and sound, in my own work on health disparities. None of these debates and discussions is resolved as regards famine, political violence, or epidemic disease, which is one reason I refer, in this essay, to general reviews. Another is simply that, although these matters are complex and beyond ready understanding (in any case, beyond mine), they are worth struggling with—especially since the views and experience of a practitioner in the midst of these events are always partial and often muddled. An acknowledgment of these limitations is all the more reason to rely on ethnographic study (once termed "participant-observation") that allows the messiness of everyday life to interrogate any grand theorizing.

This epistemological humility is increasingly common in the works of anthropologists who focus on social suffering, even if such insights aren't always quick to take hold in the course of our careers. As Unni Wikan suggests in reflecting on her four decades of ethnographic work on social suffering, "Some insights have been late in coming, and they have made me what I am now: more humble as regards the powers of anthropology to enlighten us on the human condition; more concerned that we do make use of all the knowledge that we have to help make a better world; optimistic regarding the relevance of anthropology; convinced that resonance is a way for the future. Only when we recognize the distinct humanity of the other, however inhumane and incomprehensible her actions may seem, can we hope to bridge worlds that are seemingly incommensurable" (Unni Wikan, *Resonance: Beyond the Words* [Chicago: University of Chicago Press, 2012]), 26.

[14] This "view from below," drawing on Gutiérrez and liberation theology, was what I sought to add to my mentors' work on social suffering ("On Suffering and Structural Violence: A View from Below," in *Social Suffering,* ed. A. Kleinman, V. Das, and M. Lock (Berkeley: University of California Press, 1997), 261–83. Using the liberation theologians' ideas and Johan Galtung's term, I've tried to explore "an anthropology of structural violence" (see Paul Farmer, "An Anthropology of Structural Violence," *Current Anthropology* 45, no. 3 (2004): 305–26), as have others working in this field. Barbara Rylko-Bauer and I have recently reviewed the term's use, and critiques of it, for *The Oxford Handbook of Poverty and Society* (Barbara Rylko-Bauer and Paul Farmer, "Structural Violence, Poverty, and Social Suffering," in *The Oxford Handbook of Poverty and Society*, David Brady and Linda M. Burton, eds. [Oxford: Oxford University Press, forthcoming]). My colleagues Nancy Scheper-Hughes and Philippe Bourgois have pulled together a comprehensive anthology of *Violence in War and Peace* (Oxford: Blackwell, 2004.)

[15] Although I understand some of the great debates of the era, and am interested in them, it was not the acceptance or rejection of any totalizing framework, including Marxism, that moved us most. As we sought to deliver care for those already sick, whether in Boston or Haiti or Lima, these debates did not always seem urgent or even familiar. They seemed outdated, musty, irrelevant (although they were in fact none of these). This may be owing in part to the rapid social change that is the focus of this chapter and in part to the nature of claims of causality (termed "etiology" in medicine). Claims of causality are regarded as central to clinical medicine but are deeply controversial in the social sciences. Calls to reject this or that etiologic *paradigm*, while common in discussions of politics and poverty, have been rare in medicine for the better part of a century. This may account, in part, for my own desire to avoid the obvious (economic conditions, especially poverty, often *determine* who will be sick and who will be spared and who will have access to effective

care; improving policies and "delivery platforms" for the poor are the chief tasks before a group, such as Partners In Health, and also for those who seek to build public systems to deliver such care to the poor) and to focus on how to prevent and to palliate premature suffering and death. But such matters are not always obvious even to theologians or to public servants or to political figures engaged, wittingly or not, in the war on poverty and social exclusion. Because the stakes were high, the debates were sharp; because these debates spilled into open conflict across Latin America, some theologians of liberation felt a need, rooted in times and in settings of conflict, to clarify their views of Marx or Marxist analyses. We did not feel the need, but learned from the debate. In his Introduction to Gustavo Gutiérrez's *Spiritual Writings*, Daniel Groody describes Gutiérrez's own engagement with Marxism: "As [Father Gutiérrez] addressed the problem of poverty, he saw how social sciences offered important instruments for understanding reality. Like other Latin Americans in the 1970s such as Henrique Cardoso and Enzo Faletto, he drew on the theory of dependence, which took some notions from Marxist analysis. Many have misunderstood and misinterpreted the connection between Gutiérrez, liberation theology, and Marxism, and some critics of Gutiérrez see liberation theology as some kind of 'warmed over' Marxism with a religious mask. But nothing could be further from Gutiérrez' own vision. While he did draw on certain tools of social analysis in order to understand reality, he did not, and has not, subscribed to Marxist philosophy or Marxist conclusions. Gutiérrez has affirmed consistently that the first and last line of liberation theology is against Marxism. For Marx, Christian religion was alienating. For Gutiérrez, it is liberating" (Daniel G. Groody, Introduction to *Gustavo Gutiérrez: Spiritual Writings* [Maryknoll, NY: Orbis Books, 2012], 25–26).

[16] Sally Falk Moore, "Explaining the Present: Theoretical Dilemmas in Processual Ethnography," *American Ethnologist* 14, no. 4 (1987): 727–36.

[17] The dissertation was overly long and too hastily cobbled together, but I am still proud of the published version: *AIDS and Accusation: Haiti and the Geography of Blame* (Berkeley: University of California Press, 1992, 2006). Both are peppered with allusions to Gutiérrez and other theologians of liberation, as were other accounts of those years. For example, the American Jesuits were good enough to publish a long essay, "The Power of the Poor in Haiti," its title cribbed proudly (or shamelessly) from Father Gustavo (*America* 164, no. 9 [1992]: 260–67).

[18] Similar claims had been made regarding the building of hospitals in settings of poverty, and regarding AIDS, cancer care, surgical services, and, previously, any kind of tuberculosis. Treatment for these afflictions was or is "too expensive" (or "too complex") to merit scant public treasure. But again these claims and debates are less related to the complexity of treatment than to the claim that saving poor lives is always costly in one way or another. Saving all of

these young lives in the poorest reaches of Latin American and Africa would lead, we read, to a "demographic entrapment," a state in which the success of child-survival efforts could stall, perversely, economic development. See, for example, Maurice King, "Health Is a Sustainable State," *Lancet* 336, no. 8716 (1990): 664–67; and Maurice King and C. Elliott, "Legitimate Double-Think," *Lancet* 341, no. 8846 (1993): 669–72; Maurice King and C. Elliott, "Cairo: Damp Aquib or Roman Candle?" *Lancet* 344, no. 8921 (1994): 528; and Luc Bonneux, "Rwanda: A Case of Demographic Entrapment," *Lancet* 344, no. 8938 (1994): 1689–90. These arguments held the greatest sway in the poorest countries and in those bureaucracies, home-grown and transnational, charged with allocating scarce resources. This strain of public health logic also leads straight to "the House of No," and is another reminder of the need for correctives such as a preferential option for the poor.

[19] This dilemma was laid out in both the medical literature (e.g., in Farmer et al. "The Dilemma of MDRTB in the Global Era," *International Journal of Tuberculosis and Lung Disease* 2, no. 11 [1998]: 869–76), and in the broader biosocial ones (e.g., *Infections and Inequalities* [1999 Berkeley: University of California Press, 2001]).

[20] Thomas R. Frieden et al., "Tuberculosis in New York City—Turning the Tide," *New England Journal of Medicine* 333, no. 4 (1995): 229–33.

[21] This commodification of medicine in the United States is the subject of books and studies too numerous to summarize, here or anywhere else, but is the subject of a modest review I was lucky enough to write in the anthropological literature with my friend and colleague, Barbara Rylko-Bauer (B. Rylko-Bauer and P. Farmer, "Managed Care or Managed Inequality? A Call for Critiques of Market-Based Medicine," *Medical Anthropology Quarterly* 16, no. 4 [2002]: 476–502).

[22] It's beyond the scope of this book to dissect the term "regular" tuberculosis, but other hard-to-diagnose or -treat forms of tuberculosis were also not part of the publicly funded DOTS strategy. These forms included not only disease caused by drug-resistant strains but also extrapulmonary tuberculosis and tuberculosis among children, who are harder to diagnose with the inexpensive but rudimentary diagnostic tests then used. There is a large and growing medical literature on each of these topics.

[23] The role of catastrophic illness in keeping families poor is discussed by development economists such as Jeffrey Sachs (see *The End of Poverty: Economic Possibilities of Our Time* [New York: Penguin Books, 2005]) and Matthew Bonds (see, for example, M. H. Bonds et al., "Poverty Trap Formed by the Ecology of Infectious Diseases." *Proceedings of the Royal Society of Biological Sciences* 277, no. 1685 (2010): 1185–92). See also Anirudh Krishna, *One Illness Away: Why People Become Poor and How They Escape Poverty* (New York: Oxford University Press, 2011).

²⁴ We knew from the beginning that most would be cured, and started reporting success as soon as we could document it (e.g., Farmer and J. Y. Kim, "Community-Based Approaches to the Control of Multidrug-Resistant Tuberculosis: Introducing 'DOTS-plus,'" *British Medical Journal* 317, no. 7159 [1998]: 671–74). It took years, however, to echo this in the most influential medical journals (e.g., Mitnick et al., "Community-Based Therapy for Multi-drug Resistant Tuberculosis in Lima, Peru," *New England Journal of Medicine* 348, no. 2 (2003): 119–28). It also required raising millions of dollars, since such arguments of infeasibility were always about scarce resources for delivery of care.

²⁵ Merrill Singer, *Introduction to Syndemics: A Systems Approach to Public and Community Health* (San Francisco: Jossey-Bass, 2009).

²⁶ Claims of causality about health and well-being are always difficult to make. In no instance is this more true than during times of social tumult, such as what we were witnessing in Peru, and also during the economic downturns termed recessions and depressions. The sociologist David Stuckler and the physician-epidemiologist Sanjay Basu recently examined nearly a century of data to explore the effects of investing, or failing to invest, in public health safety nets and other forms of social protection during such downturns. In the tradition of social medicine, one that complements the ethnographic approach we learned from our mentors in medical anthropology, they integrate diverse ways of knowing—quantitative data, of course, but also historical cases, personal narratives, and sociological and clinically informed analyses—about cause and consequence and experience. In investigating the "causes of the causes" of adverse health outcomes in populations from the United States (in the Great Depression and also the recent recession that began in 2007) to the Soviet Union (during the years it was becoming the Former Soviet Union) to Greece, Iceland, and the UK in the here and now, they expose many of the myths and mystifications that prop up the regnant ideologies of fiscal austerity, which often signal a contracture of social protection for those who need it most even as they mask a peculiarly bounded largesse for a fortunate few. See Sanjay Basu and David Stuckler, *The Body Economic* (New York: Basic Books, 2013).

²⁷ Gustavo Gutiérrez, *We Drink from Our Own Wells: The Spiritual Journey of a People* (1984; Maryknoll, NY: Orbis Books, 2003), 95. This is reprinted at the beginning of Chapter 4 in this book.

²⁸ Ibid., 96.

²⁹ Indeed, we have reviewed with admiration the increasing sophistication of such exercises, which are pursued by the Institute of Health Metrics and Evaluation at the University of Washington (see, for example, *The Global Burden of Disease: Generating Evidence, Guiding Policy* [Seattle: University of Washington, March 2013]).

³⁰ Those who help design and staff health services could learn a lot from listening to patients facing both illness and poverty and by reading anthropolo-

gists who chart the experience of those who are sick and poor and seeking succor. In her wonderful book *Death without Weeping: The Violence of Everyday Life in Brazil* (Berkeley: University of California Press, 1992), Nancy Scheper-Hughes explores the experience and the theodicy of poor women in northeastern Brazil, offering lessons for public health and for theologians, too. There is plenty of empirical evidence of sufferers desires for—and suggestions for building—compassionate and just health care systems. João Biehl has written compellingly about this matter in contemplating AIDS care in Brazil; Adriana Petryna has explained compensation for illness occurring after the Chernobyl disaster in the Ukraine; Veena Das has considered the Bhopal disaster through a similar lens; Arthur Kleinman has followed the trajectories of Chinese patients with mental illness; Philippe Bourgois, the trials and tribulations of heroin addicts, many of them homeless, seeking health care in two US cities. These experiences change with time, of course; they are always different for each patient and in each setting, and new therapeutic regimes reach into all corners of the world, however unequally. In an edited volume, Biehl and Petryna have brought together ethnographic studies of how health equity is playing itself out in settings around the world, reminding us all how varied the personal experience of seeking care for complex illness always is: "With our empirical lanterns, we see people refusing to be stratified out of existence and trying to be singularized out of the molds of abandonment, salvation, or rescue into which they are cast. The fine-grained ethnographic excesses of lives and stories are often smoothed over or averaged out by coarse-grained statistics and plans. Ethnographic granularity impedes generalizable knowledge, so the official story line goes. Our view, to the contrary, is that ethnography often debunks generalized knowledge, if only retrospectively or too late. The ethnographic, we argue, offers a sharper resolution of how things are, what sustains their intractability, and how they might be otherwise. People's practices of survival and inquiry challenge the analytical forms we bring to the field, forcing us to articulate more experience-near and immediately relevant conceptual work. How to operationalize ethnographic knowledge, and whether this move compromises what can and cannot be asked in the field, is a crucial and enduring question" (João Biehl and Adriana Petryna, "Critical Global Health," in *When People Come First: Critical Studies in Global Health,* ed. João Biehl and Adriana Petryna [Princeton, NJ: Princeton University Press, 2013], 17). This is another reason why, in the end, it's important to listen to those affected most directly by poverty and serious illness.

[31] Groody, Introduction, in *Gustavo Gutiérrez: Spiritual Writings,* 25.

[32] Gutiérrez, *Wells,* 98.

[33] The Millennium Development Goals, established at the United Nations Millennium Summit in September 2000 in New York City, put forth an actionable, time-bound plan for galvanizing efforts to meet the needs of

the world's poorest people. Broadly, the eight goals to be achieved by the year 2015 by participating states include an end to hunger and poverty, universal access to education, gender equity, improved child health, improved maternal health, a "bold effort" to combat HIV through integrated prevention and care, improved environmental stability, and strengthened global partnerships. For further information on the United Nations' Millennium Development Goals, see http://www.un.org/millenniumgoals/. I have drawn parallels between the Millennium Development Goals framework, which call on states to meet these goals, and the corporal works of mercy, which call on individuals, communities, and nascent religious institutions to do so, in an essay in *Notre Dame Magazine*. ("If We Fail to Act," *Notre Dame Magazine* 35, no. 3 (2006):18–27, 88–89).

[34] We documented this stunning decline within the Tomsk prison with our Russian colleagues. For an overview in the medical literature, see the report by Salmaan Keshavjee et al. ("Treating Multi-Drug Resistant Tuberculosis in Tomsk, Russia: Developing Programs that Address the Linkage between Poverty and Disease," *Annals of the New York Academy of Sciences* 2 1136 (2008):1–11).

[35] An overview of progress made toward the MDGs is offered by John McArthur, who notes that "the greatest MDG successes undoubtedly concern health" (*Foreign Affairs,* March/April 2013, 160). Other assessments focus on lack or unevenness of progress, but the trend toward longer and healthier lives has been registered worldwide. Claims of causality regarding this progress have been wildly contradictory, especially in settings of conflict and upheaval.

[36] Another, related pathology is the deepening of health disparities between rural and urban Chinese. The health economist Chunling Lu has reported that the sudden collapse of one regional rural health system lowered coverage from over 90 percent to less than 10 percent. See C. Lu, Y. Liu, and J. Shen, "Does China's Rural Cooperative Medical System Achieve Its Goals? Evidence from the China Health Surveillance Baseline Survey in 2001." *Contemporary Economic Policy* 30, no. 1 (2012): 93–112. Again, my colleagues and teachers continue to explore the impact of rapid social change (and structural violence) in works such as *Deep China: The Moral Life of the Person: What Anthropology and Psychiatry Tell Us about China Today* (Berkeley: University of California Press, 2011), a collection of essays by Arthur Kleinman and a number of his former students.

[37] For a review of these data and their provenance, see P. E. Farmer, C. T. Nutt, C. M. Wagner, C. Sekabaraga, T. Nuthulaganti, J. L. Weigel, D. Bertrand, A. Habinshuti, S. D. Mugeni, J. C. Karasi, and P. C. Drobac, "Reduced Premature Mortality in Rwanda: Lessons from Success," *British Medical Journal* (2013) 346:f65.

[38] For more on the first Haitian case, see D. A. Walton and L. C. Ivers, "The 'First' Case of Cholera in Haiti: Lessons for Global Health," *American Journal of Tropical Medicine and Hygiene* 86, no. 1 (2012): 36–38. I was invited to comment

on this paper and others addressing the Haitian epidemic, but alas, the influence of what others would call "obscure medical articles" is limited. See also P. Farmer and L. C. Ivers, "Cholera in Haiti: The Equity Agenda and the Future of Tropical Medicine," *American Journal of Tropical Medicine and Hygiene* 86, no. 1 (2012): 7–8. Case fatality data is publicly available from the Haitian Ministry of Health at http://www.mspp.gouv.ht/site/index.php.

[39] These were predictable and predicted. The claims of causality and the accusations of complicity followed the ones I'd studied decades earlier in considering AIDS. For more on social responses to cholera, see Paul Farmer, *Haiti after the Earthquake* (New York: Public Affairs, 2012).

[40] Walton and Ivers, "The First Case of Cholera in Haiti," 146.

[41] In a piece written in the first days of the epidemic that began in October 2010, we outline five complementary steps that were needed, and still are, to slow the spread of cholera (L. C. Ivers, P. Farmer, C. P. Almazor, and F. Léandre, "Five Complementary Interventions to Slow Cholera," *Lancet* 376, no. 9758 [2010]: 2048–51).

[42] For a review, see an article Jonathan Weigel and I wrote for *Americas Quarterly*, "Cholera and the Road to Modernity: Lessons from One Latin American Epidemic for Another," *America's Quarterly* 6, no. 3 (2012): 28–35.

[43] Roberto Goizueta, *Caminemos con Jesus: Toward a Hispanic/Latino Theology of Accompaniment* (Maryknoll, NY: Orbis Books, 1995), 192.

[44] Ibid., 199.

[45] For an account of efforts to provide such services to the poor in El Salvador, see Charles Clements, *Witness to War: An American Doctor in El Salvador* (New York: Bantam, 1984). Grimly similar accounts, written in Spanish and English, have emerged from across the region. See, for example, Kris Heggenhougen, "Will Primary Care Efforts Be Allowed to Succeed?" *Social Science and Medicine* 19, no. 3 (1984): 217–24.

[46] Alan Wood, *Bertrand Russell: The Passionate Skeptic: A Biography* (New York: Simon & Schuster, 1958).

[47] Groody, Introduction, in *Gutiérrez,* 18.

[48] Arthur Kleinman has pointed out that most of medicine isn't about caregiving at all. See "Caregiving: The Odyssey of Becoming More Human," *Lancet* 373, no. 9660 (2009): 292–93. But there remains in biomedicine, even in its most technologically driven specialties, reverence for the patient and, among the best physicians, a deep respect for their colleagues in the chain of care, from nurses to pharmacists to managers.

[49] See, for more on this topic, "Never Again? Reflections on Human Values and Human Rights," part of the Tanner Lectures on Human Values Series at the University of Utah. (Farmer P., "Never Again? Reflections on Human Values and Human Rights" in Petersen, G.B., ed., *The Tanner Lectures on Human Values*, Vol. 25 [Salt Lake City: University of Utah Press, 2006], 137–188).

6

The Option for the Poor
Arises from Faith in Christ

Gustavo Gutiérrez

In May 2007 the Fifth General Conference of the bishops of Latin America and the Caribbean took place in Aparecida, Brazil. The meeting explicitly and insistently situated itself within the pastoral and theological framework opened up during the years of the Second Vatican Council and the bishops' Second General Conference at Medellín, Colombia (1968). Aparecida makes the preferential option for the poor, which it considers "one of the characteristic features of the face of the Latin American and Caribbean Church," one of the central axes of its conclusions.[1]

The presence of this commitment at Aparecida owes much to the emphasis Pope Benedict XVI put on the subject in his speech at the conference. He clearly and firmly located his remarks in the appropriate theological context: "The preferential option for the poor is implicit in the Christological faith in the God who became poor for us, so as to enrich us with his poverty (cf. 2 Cor 8:9).[2] Its root is faith in Christ, which Aparecida lucidly reiterates: "This commitment is born out of our faith in Jesus Christ, the God who became human."[3]

The vision of Christian life manifested in this statement and in the practice of this commitment is, in fact, the most substantial

This essay was originally published in *Theological Studies* 70, no. 2 (2009): 317–26.

part of the contribution from the life and theological reflection of the church in Latin America to the universal church. The option for the poor took its first steps in the years before Medellín, was affirmed in the period after that conference, and was invoked in subsequent episcopal conferences and in the recent teachings of Benedict XVI and Aparecida, which have given it an impact and a place it would not have had without them.

The option for the poor is not limited to the assignment of pastoral workers to areas where the poor are found. Although it is good to see greater pastoral investment in areas of poverty, the option for the poor is more global and demanding. Some years ago Gregory Baum described it as "the contemporary form of discipleship."[4] Here I would like to present some points with respect to a perspective that goes to the marrow of Christian life. The option for the poor is deployed in three arenas: the following of Jesus, theological work, and the proclamation of the gospel. These three dimensions give the preferential option for the poor vitality and shape.

This option involves a commitment that implies leaving the road one is on, as the parable of the Good Samaritan teaches, and entering the world of the other, of the "insignificant" person, of the one excluded from dominant social sectors, communities, viewpoints, and ideas. It is a long and difficult, but necessary, process, and a precondition for authenticity. The priority of the other is a distinguishing mark of a gospel ethic, and nobody embodies this priority more clearly than the poor and the excluded. A poem by Antonio Machado speaks to us about this otherness:

> Christ teaches: your neighbor
> you will love as yourself
> but never forget that they are an other.[5]

Following Jesus

To be a Christian is to walk, moved by the Spirit, in the footsteps of Jesus. Traditionally known as *la sequela Christi*, this kind of discipleship is the root and the ultimate meaning of the preferential option for the poor.

This commitment—the expression "preferential option for the poor" is recent but its content is biblical—is an essential component of discipleship. At its core is a spiritual experience of the mystery of God who is, according to Meister Eckhart, both the "unnamable" and the "omni-namable" one. Eckhart had to reach this point in order to capture the deeper meaning of this commitment to the absent and anonymous of history. The free and demanding love of God is expressed in the commandment of Jesus to "Love one another as I have loved you" (Jn 13:34). This implies a universal love that excludes no one, and at the same time is a priority for the least ones of history, the oppressed and the insignificant. Simultaneously living out universality and preference reveals the God of love and makes present the mystery hidden for all time but now unveiled: as Paul says, the proclamation of Jesus as the Christ (see Rom 16:25–26). This is what the preferential option for the poor points to: walking with Jesus the Messiah.[6]

For this reason, Puebla reminds us that "the service of the poor is the privileged, though not exclusive, means for following Christ."[7] The lived experiences of many Christians undertaking different journeys in solidarity with the marginalized and insignificant of history have revealed that the irruption of the poor—their new presence on the historical scene— signifies a true irruption of God into our lives.

Saying this does not deprive the poor of the historical flesh of their suffering. Nor does it deprive them of the human, social, and cultural substance of their cry for justice. It is not a short-sighted "spiritualization" that forgets their human dimensions. Rather, it makes us truly see what is at stake, according to the Bible, in the commitment to one's neighbor. Precisely because we so value and respect the density of the historical event of the irruption of the poor, we are positioned to make a faith-based interpretation of this event. It is worth saying: we understand the irruption of the poor as a sign of the times, which we must scrutinize in the light of faith in order to discern the challenge of the God who has pitched his tent among us (Jn 1:14). Solidarity with the poor is the source of a spirituality, of a collective—or communal, if one prefers—journey toward God. This journey takes place in a history that the inhuman situation of the poor exposes in all its cruelty, but that also allows its possibilities and hopes to be discovered.

Following Jesus is a response to the question about the meaning of human existence; it is a global vision of our life, but it also affects life's small and everyday aspects. Discipleship allows us to see our lives in relation to the will of God and sets goals for us to strive for and realize through a daily relationship with the Lord, which implies relationships with other persons. Spirituality comes into being on the terrain of Christian practice: thanksgiving, prayer, and a commitment in history to solidarity, especially with the poorest. Contemplation and solidarity are two sides of a practice inspired by a global sense of human existence that is a source of hope and joy.

The deepest meaning of the commitment to the poor is the encounter with Christ. Echoing Matthew's pericope of the last judgment, Puebla invites us to recognize in the face of the poor "the suffering features of the face of Christ the Lord who questions and implores us."[8] This discovery calls us to personal and ecclesial conversion. Matthew's text is, without a doubt, central to Christian spirituality and provides us with a fundamental principle for discerning and finding the road of fidelity to Jesus.

In one of his homilies Archbishop Romero observed: "There is a criterion for knowing whether God is close to us or far away: all those who worry about the hungry, the naked, the poor, the disappeared, the tortured, the imprisoned—about any suffering human being—are close to God" (February 5, 1978).[9] The gesture made toward the other determines the proximity to or distance from God, and makes us understand the "why" of this judgment and the meaning of the term "spiritual" in a gospel context. "Love of God and love of neighbor have become one," says Pope Benedict in his encyclical *Deus caritas est.*[10] The identification of Christ with the poor leads us by the hand to see the fundamental unity of these two loves and makes demands on his followers. The rejection of injustice and the oppression it presupposes is anchored in faith in the God of life. This commitment has been sealed by the blood of those who, as Archbishop Romero said (and this was true in his own case), died under "the sign of martyrdom." Aparecida has movingly recognized the testimony of these Christians, referring to "the courageous witness of our men and women saints, and of those who, though not yet canonized, have radically lived the gospel and have offered their lives for Christ, for the Church, and for their people."[11]

The option for the poor is a key part of a spirituality that refuses to be a kind of oasis or, still less, an escape or a refuge in difficult times. At the same time it involves a walking with Jesus that, without being disconnected from reality and without distancing itself from the narrow paths trod by the poor, helps us keep alive our trust in the Lord and preserve our serenity when the storm gets worse.

A Hermeneutics of Hope

If the following of Jesus is marked by the preferential option for the poor, so is the understanding of the faith that unfolds from these experiences and emergencies.[12] This is the second dimension of the option for the poor that I would like to highlight.

Faith is a grace; theology is an understanding of this gift. Theology tries to say a word about the mysterious and ineffable reality that we believers call God. It is a *logos* about *theos.*

Faith is the ultimate source of theological reflection, giving theology its specificity and delimiting its territory. Its purpose is—or should be—to contribute to making the gospel present in human history through Christian testimony. A theology that is not nourished by walking Jesus' own path loses its bearings.

Those we call Fathers of the Church, for whom all theology was spiritual theology, understood this very well.

However, neither the faith nor the reflection about how the faith is being lived in community is simply an individual task. This fact makes discourse on faith a labor that is related to the preaching of the gospel, a task that gives this community its raison d'être. Every discourse on faith is born at a precise time and place and tries to respond to historical situations and questions amid which Christians live and proclaim the gospel. For that reason it is tautological, strictly speaking, to say that a theology is contextual, for all theology is contextual in one way or another. Some theologies, however, take their context seriously and recognize it; others do not.

The theology of liberation, like other reflections on the Christian message that arise from the world of those considered socially insignificant, postulates that discourse on faith must recognize and emphasize its relationship with human history and people's everyday lives, especially the challenge of poverty manifested there. This relationship with history and the challenge of poverty implies an important change in the task of theology. Although we have long pidgeonholed poverty as a social issue, our perception of poverty is now deeper and more complex, and no longer limited to its economic dimension (as important as this may be). Instead, we now understand that being poor means being rendered socially insignificant owing to ethnic, cultural, gender, and/or economic factors. Poverty's inhumane and anti-evangelical character, as Medellín and Puebla put it, and its final outcome of early and unjust death make it totally clear that poverty goes beyond the socioeconomic sphere to become a global human problem and therefore a challenge to living and preaching the gospel. Poverty thereby becomes a theological question, and the option for the poor makes us aware of it and provides a way to think about the issue.

Like all challenges to faith, the condition of the poor questions and interrogates while providing principles and categories that open up new approaches to understanding and deepening the Christian message. It is critical to consider the counterpart and the other side of every question. Theological work consists of confronting challenges face-to-face, no matter how radical they may be, recognizing the signs of the times that contain them, and discerning in them, by the light of faith, the new field of faith interpretation being presented; thus will our thinking about the faith and our speech about God speak to the people of our age.

From this perspective, the preferential option for the poor plays an important role in theological reflection. As is stated in the classic formula *fides quaerens intellectum*, theology is faith seeking understanding. Given that faith "operates through charity" (Gal 5:6), theology is a reflection that tries to accompany a people in their sufferings and joys, their commitments, frustrations, and hopes, both in becoming aware of the social universe in which they live and in their determination to understand better their own cultural tradition. A theological language that neglects unjust suffering and does not loudly proclaim the right of each and every person to happiness remains shallow and betrays the God of whom it speaks, the God of the beatitudes.

In the end, theology—all theology—is a hermeneutics of hope, an understanding of the reasons we have to hope. Hope is, in the first place, a gift from God. Accepting that gift opens followers of Jesus to the future and to trust. Seeing theological work as an attempt to understand the reasons for hope becomes more demanding when it begins with the situation of the poor and continues in solidarity with them. God's gift is not an easy hope. But as fragile as it may seem, it is capable of planting roots in the world of social insignificance, in the world of the poor, and of breaking out and remaining creative and alive even in the midst of difficult situations. Nonetheless, hoping is not waiting; rather it should lead us to actively resolve to forge reasons for hope.

Paul Ricoeur says that theology is born at the intersection of "a space of experience" and "a horizon of hope." It is a space where Jesus invites us to follow him in encountering the other, especially the "smallest" of his brothers and sisters—and to follow him in the hope that in this encounter, which is open to every person, believer or unbeliever, we will stand within the horizon of service to the other and in communion with the Lord.

A Prophetic Announcement
of the Good News

The preferential option for the poor that grounds theological attempts to forge reasons for hope is also an essential component of the prophetic proclamation of the gospel, a proclamation that includes the connection between justice and God's gratuitous love. Working so that the excluded might become agents of their own destiny is an important part of this proclamation.

We cannot enter into the world of the poor, who live in an inhumane situation of exclusion, without becoming aware of the liberating and humanizing dimension of the good news. And for that very reason we cannot fail to hear the gospel's cry for justice as well as for equality among all human beings. This is a core theme in the prophetic tradition of the First Testament, which we meet again in the middle of the Sermon on the Mount as a command summarizing and giving meaning to the life of the believer: "Seek first the kingdom of God and his righteousness" (Mt 6:33).

The heart of Jesus' message is the proclamation of the love of God that is expressed in the proclamation of his kingdom. The kingdom is the final meaning of history; its total fulfillment takes place beyond history, and at the same time it is present from this moment on. The gospels speak to us precisely of its closeness to us today. The parables of the kingdom point to a kingdom that is "already" present but "not yet" fully realized. For this reason the Kingdom of God manifests itself as a gift, a grace, but also as a task, a responsibility.

The life of the disciple of Jesus is situated within the framework of the sometimes tense but always fertile relationship between free gift and historical commitment; thus our talk about the kingdom we accept in faith is situated within the same framework. The passage from the beatitudes of Matthew contains a promise of the kingdom to all who, upon accepting in their daily lives the free gift offered to them, become Jesus' disciples. In the gospels the kingdom is discussed through expressions and images of great biblical richness: land, consolation, thirst, mercy, the vision of God, and divine filiation. The dominant theme of these images is life, life in all its aspects. As for the requirements of discipleship, they are stated fundamentally in the first and most critical blessing: being poor in spirit. The other blessings offer variations and shades of the first. Disciples are those who make the promise of the kingdom their own, placing their lives in God's hands. Recognizing the gift of the kingdom sets them free vis-à-vis all other goods. And it opens them up to the mission of evangelization, which is linked to "remembering the poor" (Gal 2: 10), according to the advice Paul received in Jerusalem.

Theological thinking in recent decades, as well as various texts of the magisterium, has insisted on the relationship between evangelization and the promotion of justice. Examples include the Medellín conference, the Roman Synod of 1971, *Evangelii nuntiandi* by Paul VI, and a number of speeches by John Paul II. One can see in these documents an orientation toward these two aspects that is increasingly global and unitary.

The promotion of justice is seen more and more as an essential part of proclaiming the gospel. Such promotion is, of course, not all there is to evangelization, but neither is it situated only on the threshold of the proclamation of the good news, for it is not preevangelization as was once held. Rather, it constitutes an essential part of the proclamation of the kingdom, even though it does not exhaust its content. The road has been long, but its current formulation clearly avoids impoverishing separations as well as possible confusions of the two. Benedict XVI, in a text cited by the Aparecida conference, stated that "evangelization has always been joined to human promotion and authentic Christian liberation."[13]

In addition, solidarity with the poor also sets forth a fundamental demand: the recognition of the full human dignity of the poor and their situation as daughters and sons of God. In fact, the conviction grows amid the poor that, like all human beings, they have the right to take control of the reins of their lives. This conviction is not a theoretical proposition or a rhetorical appeal, but rather a truly difficult and costly, but obligatory, lifestyle. And it is urgent, if we take into account the fact that today in Latin America and the Caribbean there are those who attempt to sow skepticism about the capacity of the poor to achieve the transformation of society by promoting what they call "the only way to think." They try to persuade the poor that in the face of the new and inescapable realities of globalization, the international economic situation, and political and military unipolarity, they have no choice but to accept the vision those realities express and to radically change the direction of their demands.

There is no true commitment to solidarity with the poor if one sees them merely as people passively waiting for help. Respecting their status as those who control their own destiny is an indispensable condition for genuine solidarity. For that reason the goal is not to become, except in cases of extreme urgency or short duration, the "voice of the voiceless" as is sometimes said—undoubtedly with the best of intentions—but rather in some way to help ensure that those without a voice find one. Being an agent of one's own history is for all people an expression of freedom and dignity, the starting point and a source of authentic human development. The historically insignificant were—and still are in large part—the silent in history.

For this reason it is important to note that the option for the poor is not something that should be made only by those who are not poor. The poor themselves are called to make an option that gives priority to the "insignificant" and oppressed. Many do so, but it must be recognized that not all commit themselves to their sisters and brothers by race, gender, social class, or culture. The path the poor must take to identify with the least of society will be different from that of people belonging to other social strata, but it is a necessary and important step toward becoming subjects of their own destiny.

It is good to specify that the preferential option for the poor, if it aims at the promotion of justice, equally implies friendship with the poor and among the poor. Without friendship there is neither authentic solidarity nor a true sharing. In fact, it is a commitment to specific people. Aparecida says in this regard, "Only the closeness that makes us friends allows us to profoundly appreciate the values of the poor today, their legitimate desires, and their own way of living the faith. The option for the poor should lead us to friendship with the poor."[14]

In this chapter, then, I have distinguished three dimensions of the preferential option for the poor—spiritual, theological, and evangelical—so that I might address them one by one and be able to sketch the characteristic profile of each. But it is clear that if we separate them, we distort and impoverish them. They are interwoven and nourish each other; when they are treated as watertight compartments, they lose their meaning and power.

The preferential option for the poor constitutes a part of following Jesus that gives ultimate meaning to human existence, and that gives us as believers "reason to hope" (1 Pt 3:15). It helps us see the understanding of faith as a hermeneutics of hope, an interpretation that must be constantly enacted and reenacted throughout our lives and human history, building up reasons for hope. Finally, the option for the poor propels us to discover appropriate paths for a prophetic proclamation of the Kingdom of God, a communication that respects and creates social justice, communion, fraternity, and equality among people.

—Translated by Robert Lasalle-Klein with
James Mickeloff and Susan Sullivan

Notes

[1] V Conferencia General del Episcopado Latinoamericano y del Caribe, May 13–31, 2007, Aparecida, Brazil, Documento de Aparecida, no. 391, http://www.usccb.org/latinamerica/english/Documento_Conclusivo_Aparecida.pdf (accessed May 4, 2013).

[2] Pope Benedict XVI, Address of His Holiness Benedict XVI to the Bishops of Latin America and the Caribbean, Shrine of Aparecida, May 13, 2007, no. 3, http://www.vatican.va/holy_father/benedict_xvi/speeches/2007/may/documents/hfben-xvi_spe_20070513_conference-aparecida_en.html (accessed March 24, 2009).

[3] Documento de Aparecida, no. 392.

[4] Gregory Baum, *Essays in Critical Theology* (Kansas City, MO: Sheed & Ward, 1994), 67.

[5] Antonio Machado, "Campos de Castilla" (Proverbios y cantares XLII), *Poesías Completas* (Madrid: Espasa-Calpe, 1979), 273.

[6] The source for this position is biblical, but the immediate reference is the well-known phrase of John XXIII: "the church of all, and particularly the church of the poor" (John XXIII, "Radio message to all the Christian faithful one month before the opening of the Second Vatican Ecumenical Council" [September 11, 1962], http://www. vatican.va/holy_father/john_xxiii/speeches/1962/documentsMj-xxiii_spe_19620911_ecumenical-council_it.html [accessed March 24, 2009]).

[7] III Conferencia General del Episcopado Latinoamericano, January 28, 1979, Documento de Puebla, no. 1146, www.uca.edu.ar/esp/sec-pec/esp/docs-celam/pdf/puebla.pdf (accessed May 4, 2013).

[8] Ibid., no. 31.

[9] Archbishop Oscar Romero, "La Iglesia cuya debilidad se apoya en Cristo: Quinto domingo del tiempo ordinario, 5 de febrero de 1978. Isaías 58: 7–10,1 Corintios 1:1–5, Mateo 5: 13–16," *La palabra viva de Monseñor Romero* (Koinonía), http://servicioskoinonia.org/romero/homilias/A/780205.htm (accessed April7, 2009).

[10] Benedict XVI, *Deus caritas est* no. 15, http://www.vatican.va/holy_father/benedict_xvi/encyclicals/documents/hf_ben–xvi_enc20051225_deus-caritas-est_en. html (accessed May 4, 2013).

[11] Documento de Aparecida, no. 98.

[12] A few decades ago Marie-Dominique Chenu accurately stated, "Finally, theological systems are nothing but an expression of spiritualities" (Marie-Dominique Chenu, *Le Saulchoir: Une* école *de théologie* [Etiolles, France: Le Saulchoir, 1937]). Spirituality is, in effect, the key unifying force of theology.

[13] Benedict XVI, Address at Aparecida, no. 3; see also no. 26. A little further on (no. 4) he says that the church is called to be "a lawyer for justice and a defender of the poor." See also Documento de Aparecida, no. 395.

[14] Documento de Aparecida, no. 398.

7

Reimagining Accompaniment

An Interview with Paul Farmer
and Gustavo Gutiérrez

Interviewed by Daniel G. Groody
University of Notre Dame, October 24, 2011

*Dan Groody: How did you come to know Gustavo, and what influence
did he have on you?*

Paul Farmer: I came to know Gustavo, as many others did,
through his writings. I had become very interested in the events
in Central America after Archbishop Romero was murdered in
El Salvador. At first, my interest in liberation theology emerged
from an academic perspective, but once I traveled to Haiti, it
meant a lot more to me. I was surrounded in central Haiti by
something that felt violent and oppressive—namely, deep poverty
and the tail end of the Duvalier dictatorship. Violence was both
everyday and structural—in the words of one woman I met: it
was the fight for wood, and water, and food. The people with
whom I stayed lived in a squatter settlement because some of
them had been displaced by a hydroelectric dam. This was their
experience of structural violence.

How does one make sense of this landscape of violence as a
twenty-three-year-old American? I read a lot about the history
of Haiti. I read great books that were about Haitian culture, including one about that particular valley where I lived, but I really
took a lot of consolation from Gustavo's work. I felt that I knew

you very well. Gustavo, even before I ever went to Peru. When I finally did go to Peru, I found myself at the end of a civil war, a cholera epidemic, and in the beginning of an epidemic of drug-resistant tuberculosis. The clinical skills that I had cultivated over the years in Haiti and at Harvard were useful there. But there was still so much to be learned about poverty right there in Lima. And so, Gustavo and I became friends.

When you think back on Gustavo's writings, was there anything in particular that reached out to you?

PF: What was I then, twenty-five or a bit older? I look back at my own books and at my doctoral dissertation, which I was writing in the late eighties and they already are full of "Gustavo-isms" and quotations. In my first book, I used *On Job* and *A Theology of Liberation.* Looking back, I think it was the humility that struck me—Gustavo's understanding that fighting poverty is a humbling kind of engagement, even for a well-known theologian. In some ways, it is easier for a doctor because if you make a preferential option for the poor, you are inexorably led to addressing health disparities.

Paul, were there any stories in particular that really crystallized this for you, or was it part of your background? Obviously, there was openness [to working on behalf of the poor], but what in particular led you in this direction?

PF: As I mentioned already, from the start I've been working with Haitian colleagues. In my first year there, we went to a squatter settlement in the Artibonite Valley. In northern Lima, the squatter settlements were formed from a combination of push-pull forces—violence, civil war, agrarian collapse, etc. In this particular place in central Haiti, the people that I lived with had been displaced by a development project—a hydroelectric dam. There was this great irony that was not satisfying to contemplate. There was a great pathos in thinking that somewhere in the world, people had dreamed up this dam to help the poor, and it wasn't helping the ones I met.

So in those first years in rural Haiti, I worked with six other people more or less my age. Within five years, three of them were dead. One died right after childbirth with a nineteenth-century complication of childbirth called puerperal sepsis, which I had never seen. In fact, I've still never seen it at Harvard. It is a bacterial infection primarily caused by contamination of the genital tract during delivery, which can be fatal to mother and infant. So she died. Another young woman whom I became very close to started having signs of psychosis. But hers was not a mental illness. She had cerebral malaria, and she died, misdiagnosed, in a psychiatrist's waiting room. A third one, a young man I traipsed all over this part of Haiti with while doing a health census, drank impure water, got typhoid, and died on the operating room table of the general hospital, again in pain and misery.

Setbacks and defeats like these kept bringing me back to Gustavo's writings and to those of other liberation theologians; I needed them so that I could go on working there. Unfortunately, every year there has been punctuated by such dramas. They're different dramas now. These days in that area of Haiti, we don't lose many young women to puerperal sepsis. We don't lose people to cerebral malaria—at least not very often—and we don't lose as many people to typhoid. But now there's cholera. In medicine and public health there are some victories, and I'm grateful for them, but when you're siding with the poor and making a preferential option to serve them, you're going to come up against defeats, both theirs and yours, again and again.

When you look at the things you've read, whether on social service or other topics, what in particular distinguishes Gustavo's writings?

PF: Gustavo's writing has a few characteristics that I'd like to share with students. One is its disciplined humility. Theology doesn't lack for arrogance. From the outsider's point of view, the very idea of writing about the theory of Godhead, not to mention the grand authoritative pronouncements of theologians over the centuries, hardly seems an exercise in modesty. It's funny, but I've never asked Gustavo how he writes theology. We talk about what's happening in Peru, or in Haiti, or work that he's doing, or various struggles. So maybe it's time I asked him: How do you manage to write theology that's marked by such humility?

Another characteristic is its discipline. His theology is always moving from beneath. That's what he's been doing for five decades now: thinking, living, working, and reflecting with the people who know most about poverty—those who live in poverty themselves. Medicine is the same way. If you want to understand an illness, examine it from the point of view of the poor. Just as we can push humility into a discipline, we can also push methodological humility, humility about the claims of causality we make. In Gustavo's work, I see the great value of approaching these discussions and debates from below.

Of course, as Gustavo himself has put it, there is a profound spirituality that comes from humble reflection on misfortune. I feel that Gustavo's readings are just as relevant as they were when I was a young man becoming a doctor working with the poor.

Finally, if I may turn to him directly and ask: Gustavo, you work in the exalted realms of theology and also in the nitty-gritty of the daily struggles of poor people trying to survive. How do you span these worlds so humbly and effectively?

Gustavo Gutiérrez: Well, I will try to take, metaphorically, some distance to try to answer your question. The deepest human, and by consequence, Christian, issue is the suffering of the innocent. When we are faced with this question daily, as in the case of the little boys and girls in my parish in Lima, we need to become aware of our weaknesses and of the difficulties in sincerely responding to these questions. Silence is only one subject of theology; the first premise in theology is to speak about the absence of this question of the suffering of the innocent. Paul, you were right about the humility of theology. One part of this humility is diligence, because while we do not have answers to many questions, we can do something. Even if we cannot explain situations of suffering, we can be close to the people suffering.

Liberation theology begins with the question: How do you say to the poor, "God loves you"? This is our call to witness as followers of Jesus, although the question is greater than our capacity to answer it. To be Christians, we must follow Jesus by walking with the poor. In the Bishop's Conference of Aparecida, Pope Benedict XVI's inaugural address recalled that "the preferential option for the poor is implicit in the Christological faith in the God who became poor for us, so as to enrich us with his poverty." The preferential option is implicit in the Christian verdict. It means not only to be close to the human aspect of the poor person, but must also be linked to ethological faith and borne through the faith in Christ. Faith in Christ is not only a human issue, but rather a global issue.

I think very much about the witness of your [Farmer's] work: accompaniment which is reflection. I had in my medical school one very good professor of physiology who said often, "Remember, nothing is more practical than a good theory." I think he made things very clear. But theology is both *theoria* and *praxis*. The reflection, the *theoria*, is very important to understand issues, situations of suffering, reasons for poverty, and so forth. We must, though, as people working in theology, be practical also because in parts of the world theology is very practical.

Praxis is a person's daily life. In the context of liberation and the framework of liberation theology, we understand theological reflection as coming from *praxis* and moving towards *praxis*. This is not a new concept. Theology in the first centuries [of the Christian era] was very concretely directed toward theology made in order to help Christians to be Christians and to help the church to build a church.

After some centuries, theology was named after wisdom, "sophia." In Spanish, because of our Latin source, we have a very important play of words about wisdom. Wisdom in Spanish is *sabiduría*. *Sabiduría* has the same root as *saber*: "to know," or "to know who is testing." I think this is a type of theology. At the same time, every theology, in order to be relevant, must dialogue with contemporary thought as we are doing here.

But there are other aspects of the same issue. If we say the preferential option for the poor is preferential, that is to say, literally a *preference*, we must also recall a key point in the gospels—the universal love of God. No one, poor or nonpoor, is outside of the love of God. By preferential, we say that the poor are the first, but this is an ordinal number. There is a second, third, and fourth, and while the poor are the first, the others are second. This recorded universality of God's love goes first to the weakest.

For example, you write about the preferential option for the poor for people suffering with tuberculosis, which is a big problem everywhere in my country of Peru. Ninety percent of liberation theology is centered on the preferential option for the poor, and 10 percent deals with various other matters. Typically, I am very sensitive to manners of practicing the preferential option, and I have seen that medicine is very close to suffering. When I was young, I studied medicine in the Lima hospital for some years, and so encountered the magnitude of the suffering of the sick.

Theology must take seriously the challenge of reflection about suffering, and it must dwell upon the ways to help these people. One needs physical hands certainly, but friendship too, as you mentioned. If we lack friendship with the poor, we cannot perform an option for the poor. The option for the poor is not an option for a certain social class, gender, or culture. It's an option for the completeness of the person.

Paul, I find that your work very much underscores this point of approaching the wholeness of the person. An ill and suffering person has not only physical needs, but the need for understanding and recognition as well. This multifaceted view is very important when speaking about liberation theology. We strive passionately for social, economic, political, and cultural liberation, as well as liberation from sin. Liberation is a complex verdict. These various dimensions, though, are not many different liberations but dimensions of only one liberation.

I want to highlight two points. First, liberation from sin is liberation from the refusal to love. We are very creative in different manners of sinning—there are many ways to refuse to love. The other point in liberation theology is to accompany, to be close, and to mitigate the suffering of individuals. This is an expression of love, with the intention being to show that *you* are relevant for *me*. This kind of theology is not pragmatic theology, it is practical theology. Thomas Aquinas asked the question: Is theology speculative to the utmost degree? He said, yes, it certainly is. It is practical also. I think that Aquinas shows us a way to approach theology that is speculative but must also be linked to the practical aspect. I will be very happy to have many other ways to put in practice the preferential option for the poor.

In the gospel of Matthew, it is said, "Not everyone who says to me, 'Lord, Lord' will enter the kingdom of Heaven, but only he who does the will of my Father who is in Heaven" (7:21). To do the will of God, it is not enough to say, "Lord, Lord," but we must live in *praxis* as persons walking toward the Kingdom of God. In liberation theology, we have hundreds of expressions for this. By consequence, we must creatively imagine these many manners of walking towards the kingdom. To conclude, taking Paul's point, I think we must recognize our hindrances, rather than our abilities, towards fully comprehending and enacting the question which is the foundation of liberation theology: How do you say to the poor, "God loves you"?

Paul, in your writings, you say that illnesses affect people of varied social classes differently. In the world today, many poor are dying from sicknesses that no longer threaten the rich. To be protected from these diseases, you need to be someone with political, economic, or social power, but the poor who are insignificant are dying. This was very clear in the fight of the former president of South Africa against AIDS. I think poverty is certainly a health problem, a physical problem, a social problem, and a political problem. It is a human problem because the poor are persons and persons have all of these dimensions.

Paul, You've been to Rwanda, Haiti, Lima, and many other places in the world and are immersed in the reality of these darkest of places. Where do you find hope in the midst of all this?

PF: Well, Gustavo has written a lot about the theology of hope, so I want to hear his response. Speaking of darkness, let's not forget prison, where there is a lot of suffering, and some of it the suffering of the innocent, although I also take care of a lot of people who are guilty as charged. Something that gives me hope is that a lot of the patients I see get better. Let's go back in time. In the early twentieth century, and maybe even when Father Gustavo suffered from osteomyelitis as a teenager, we didn't have the tools that allow us to diagnose and treat such problems effectively, whether in Rwanda, Haiti, Malawi, Lima, or parts of the United States. We have those tools now, including antibiotics, and can hope to use them justly and effectively.

Another thing that gives me hope is—using language from Partners In Health—a serious equity plan that procures medications and makes them available to those who need them regardless of ability to pay. To push the preferential option for the poor, you would not *just* make it available to them even if they couldn't pay for it. You would say, "These are our chief patients and the ones we most care about—the ones who can't pay, the ones who are poor, the ones who endure desperate burdens of suffering. Making that commitment and linking it to procurement and delivery of services requires accompaniment." If you accompany them all the way through, they get better. Who wouldn't be hopeful in modern medicine? If you apply modern medicine justly with a preferential option for the poor plus accompaniment, you have the most hopeful endeavor you could imagine. The great majority of your patients would respond to these interventions. To use a very crass Americanism, you get a lot of "bang for the buck" with modern medicine in a setting of great poverty.

You work in government and policy where you recognize that a lot can be done, but it's not being done. In the midst of that situation, what do you do?

PF: We discussed this yesterday with Father Gustavo. If we assume that we cannot take the idea of accompaniment or a preferential option for the poor to the halls of power where decisions are made and policies are set, then we engage in a self-fulfilling prophecy. If we assume we can't, we won't. If we assume that we might be able to make headway on these problems by working not only directly with the people we serve who are living in poverty, but with other people who may be policymakers, by giving them information and the chance to play a constructive role and to undertake long-term commitments—if we assume that we might change their hearts, we have to do that. Only weariness or arbitrarily saying, "I'm not part of this world," would allow us not to do this. When I say "us," I mean physicians and global health activists. I don't necessarily mean Father Gustavo, or an epidemiologist working in Lima, say, and I'm not saying that everybody has the same obligation to do this. Some of us do, though, and if we work as members of teams of communities, we're more likely to make headway. I'm even optimistic about that endeavor—making people in positions of power see that accompaniment is a better model than the ones that are generally applied now.

Creating Boundaries:
Failures of Imagination

Paul, you said that Catholicism in your younger years slowed you down in many ways from making these connections between the world as it is and the world as we are called to be. Gustavo, you have said again and again that the central challenge is: How do we speak about God from the context of poverty? I think of Steve Jobs who said that when he

was thirteen he stopped going to church because he saw the cover of Life
*magazine of starving people in Africa. For a lot of people, religion and
poverty create this giant disconnect but at some point, each of you saw a
connection between the two. Can you say more about that?*

PF: I can definitely say that I was not as reflective at thirteen
as Steve Jobs. It didn't seem relevant because, you know, you go
to church because your grandmothers want you to, and then
you go through First Communion and Confirmation for the
same reason. I didn't understand the relationship between this
Catholic world and something like, say, a famine that made the
cover of *Life* magazine. If you had told me, as a teenager living in
Florida, that the United States had occupied Haiti militarily for
nineteen years, I would have had no idea what that meant, and
that occurred in the twentieth century. We create the borders of
our world as humans, and then forget history and connection. I
know that some adults are worse at this than teenagers. One of
the things that happens in medicine is that professionals are so
busy that they limit the borders of their world to wherever they
are and to whichever patients get to them in their hospitals or
clinics. That's *their* world of the sick. But it's not true of the sick.
There are many who never receive good medical care. The world
of the sick is vast, just like the world of suffering, and as Gustavo
said, these two are obviously linked. The world of the sick is part
of the world of the suffering.

   You asked me when that really clicked for me. It actually
clicked before Haiti. I'm proud to say that it clicked in college,
but it was again a story of opening up one's mind and eyes. It
just so happened that I was interested in migrant farm workers.
It's impossible to grow up in rural Florida and not have some
contact with migrant farm workers, but it is possible to have
very little. In college, when I was becoming interested in the
world as you are supposed to do in college, I studied abroad
in France, and I started writing. Learning to write for student
publications was very helpful to me. In learning to think critically and do what I would humbly enough call research, I began

writing about migrant farm workers. I met some people whose involvement with this struggle arose from their religious motivations. They were liberation theologians, in fact. They were part of the Friends of the United Farm Worker Movement, and I thought, wow, that's a different species of Catholic. When I went to Haiti, I was eager to learn more about this. When one is twenty or so, this is a really good time to insist with a little bit of rigor that the boundaries of their world are not ours to choose. We don't live in the first world, the second world, or the third world. We live in *one* world. Many liberation theologians, especially you, Gustavo, have insisted on this point. You just can't carve things up along the lines of gender or ethnicity or nationality. There is a world we live in, and there are persons in that world. We need to reach out across these barriers and to make genuine, authentic ties with people. There is no excuse to not do that in medicine. You've made a distinction between pragmatic and practical, which I will have to go and study because I thought pragmatism was a good thing, but I guess that Augustine must have thought it somehow crass. Practicality, on the other hand, is what medicine should be all about—the most practical services. A friend of mine says that the ministry of being a doctor or nurse means that you're thinking about people's health and well-being and how to use these life-saving tools for them. At the same time, we know there is both a personal and a spiritual component to this work.

When I was living in Peru, within a twelve-hour span, I went from a prison in the middle of a cholera epidemic in Lima to playing golf at a country club in Miami. Both of you experience this same tension between the academic world and the grassroots work. How do you span this difference? What gives you vision and perspective as you go back and forth between the two worlds?

PF: Thirty years ago, I found the brusque juxtaposition of those worlds harsh, and I was not mature enough to span them effectively. It leads to, if I may use a very scientific word, crankiness, which is not a spiritually profound way of reflecting on disparities in the world. It does take time to cultivate maturity. It's still hard. One of the great things that I think anybody can do is, again, raise awareness of the knowledge that you do not create the boundaries of your world. You can arbitrarily shut yourself off, which is required sometimes for reflection and silence as some sort of retreat. I understand that need for retreat.

There's another way we have to deny that there are different worlds. Our clinics might be situated in what people call the third world, but they're not third world clinics. We keep trying to build them better and literally make them more reflective of our respect for patients. That means they need to be clean, well-ordered, well-stocked, maybe even beautiful. When you open yourself up to the suffering of another, especially if you're trained in medicine, you understand that their sickness is not just a disease, like cholera, for example. It's also not having clean water, or they wouldn't have cholera, not having a house. Their kids aren't in school, they don't have enough to eat or to feed their families, et cetera et cetera. Sickness is a part of that person's world; it's not that sickness is a world separate from these other things. Similarly, it takes energy to sustain the fiction that Miami and Lima are in different worlds. The differences between those places do not amount to an ethically meaningful distinction.

I'm an infectious disease doctor, so let me put it this way. Such distinctions are certainly not meaningful to the microbes. Look what happened in Haiti in 2010–2011. After a cholera strain was introduced into Haiti from abroad, a runaway cholera epidemic spread across the whole country, and then the region, in less than a year. The microbes aren't buying the boundaries. It takes some energy for us to pretend that those boundaries are absolute, or that we can use them to protect us from this world of want. Once we realize that we can't do that anymore, the next step is to say, "Okay, what can I do to make a contribution on both sides of these socially constructed borders?"

Gratuity: Guilt and Innocence

One point that I would like to hear a little more about, Gustavo, is the gratuity of God as the impetus of the option for the poor. Most people tend to think of the option for the poor as just a social vision, but for you it's a social vision that emerges from a spirituality.

GG: Well, Paul was speaking before about the relationship of praxis and reflection. The thing I find most stimulating in my faith is my work. The question is not about the implementation of our ideas, but rather how to recognize and respond to new challenges in our faith. About gratuity—it is a central notion in the biblical message. God loves *you* first. It is in the First Letter of John: "In this is love, not that we loved God, but that he loved us, and sent his Son as the atoning sacrifice for our sins" (1 Jn 4:10). We are loved gratuitously in spite of our transgressions, and we also desire to love others in spite of their transgressions. This notion is very important because it is very human. Our primary aspiration is to be loved, not because of our interests but because of our service. This is the integral notion of the preferential option for the poor.

The preferential option is not opposed to justice. While the option for the poor certainly has dimensions of justice, it is not enough to simply fight for justice. The right to justice has a limit, but the Bible teaches that love has no limit. In the short, very beautiful letter of Paul to Philemon, he sends the former slave, Onesimus, back, saying, "Having confidence in your obedience, I write to you, knowing that you will do even beyond what I say" (Phlm 1:21). It is not enough to simply uphold individual rights—it must be more than that. This is also an important notion in the Book of Job, in Paul, and later on in Augustine and Martin Luther. We also recall this notion in liberation theology.

PF: I see it most in our work with prisoners in Rwanda, Siberia, and Haiti. I have to confess that we are not explicitly thinking about gratuity, but it's definitely in there. More than 90 percent of the prisoners in Haiti have never been tried, and in any case, the whole notion of innocence and guilt is not very helpful to the clinicians. I would say that innocence or the contrary is irrelevant in prison medicine, because judgement is not the purpose for the presence of the doctors and the nurses there. People go to prison as punishment, not for punishment. This idea reminds us that conditions have to be humane. Some critics of our work say, "You give better care to prisoners than to people who aren't in prison." If that's true, what of it? If you apply the preferential option for the poor to prisons, you might even say that, since prisoners are by definition deprived, conditions in prison should be better than when people's liberty is not constrained. I could easily live with that, although it wouldn't be a popular position to take.

In Rwanda, most of the people we cared for inside the prison system in our first years there were guilty of participating in the genocide. But, the people who invited us in to take care of them were the surviving victims of the genocide, many of whom now occupy government positions. We said, "Yes, we would be honored to take care of prisoners, even those guilty of heinous crimes, because they are in prison as punishment, not for punishment." In Rwanda as in Siberia, I did not know the crimes of the prisoners I saw as a doctor. Some of them had very long sentences, but I was not there to pass judgment on them as detainees. Our concern was to deliver quality medical services to them because they are human. The notion of gratuity as I read it in your writing can be very helpful, especially inside the practice of medicine with people who have done bad things. I do not know if all of the other doctors and nurses working with us feel that way.

We Drink from Our Own Wells

Some doctors do similar things to what you do, but without being raised in theology or gratuity. Is there a way in which your own spirituality plays a role in what you do?

PF: I have no doubt that it does. What really encourages me, however, is that there are people who, to use one of Gustavo's expressions, drink from their own wells, which are very different from those that I have drunk from. As a teacher at Harvard, I meet students from all over the world from a multitude of faith traditions, as well as those who insist, as I once did, that they do not have a faith tradition. I have found that the notions of justice, fair play, equity, and restitution are a way to engage almost anyone in this work.

Partners In Health, for example, is not a religious organization. It is a secular organization. That does not mean that people in it cannot derive inspiration, spiritual or otherwise, from liberation theology. I would say that most of the people I work with inside Partners In Health who are neither Catholic nor Christian actually do derive inspiration from liberation theology. They may have different reasons and different backgrounds, but it does not seem to me that liberation theology is closed to them. They can still make a preferential option for the poor.

Gustavo, if someone were to ask you what wells you drink from, other than your concern for the human being, what would you add?

GG: This sentence, "We Drink from Our Own Wells," comes from St. Bernard of Clairvaux. It was a very beautiful idea, to root spirituality in our own experience, and I use this as a metaphor which is especially relevant to Latin America. My intention was not to say that it is good only for Latin America, but to emphasize that we live in the context of a local situation. Our drinking is from this very concrete reality. Fundamentally, the manners are the same, but concretely, we depend on other situations, and many aspects of the idea are very local in many aspects. This was the idea behind naming my book in this way.

Do either of you, Paul or Gustavo, want to add anything to round out these issues?

GG: You mentioned something previously about hope—well, hope is not the solution. Hope is not the solution because it is possible to change a situation. Hope is rather a grace, a gift. We need to receive this gift, not only for faith but also for charity. This means creating reasons for hope today.

For me, one way to understand theology is as a higher conception of hope. Hope is one attitude, but our main conviction is the love of God present in our lives. In the First Letter of Peter, it is said, "be always ready to give an answer to everyone who asks you a reason concerning the hope that is in you." You need to explain, and to give the reasons of your hope. In this, we need to create, rather than ask when confronted by suffering, what are the reasons to hope? Chapter 32 in Jeremiah is very good for this. We must also create with the sense of very concrete commitments. This way we are creating reasons for hope. The attitude of hope is conviction of the presence of the love of God in our lives, and living according to this by creating reasons of hope for other persons and certainly for ourselves.

PF: I'm smiling because yesterday I tried to show you pictures of a hospital that we built in northern Rwanda with our partners and you started talking about Jeremiah 32. I'm embarrassed to say that I don't know what's in Jeremiah 32, but when you say, to create reasons for hope, and not just assume it's something that we don't have to look for, I have to say that is one of the reasons we build our facilities. It is not only to provide medical services.

The reason I wanted you to look at this hospital is because we built it as a reason for hope. It was built at a former military base. After the genocide and the war, we asked the government, "Can we raze this military base, and build a temple of healing there?" We did. It was explicitly in some sense to give hope to the people there who had never had a doctor before. Now they have twenty doctors and sixty nurses, and it's a beautiful hospital. It also gives us hope. We build our own reasons for hope, and in a way, in medicine, that is drinking from your own wells too. That's part of what I meant when I said, "One of the wells that we get to drink from in medicine is having the tools that we need to serve the sick." So, how do you make a preferential option for the poor who are critically ill if you don't have a hospital and you don't have medicines and you don't have the staff? I don't think we should try to do that.

Hope in Suffering: Jeremiah and Job

I want to ask Gustavo to say a bit more regarding this theme of hope and where we draw our hope. You mentioned the thirty-second chapter of Jeremiah which speaks about the actions we should take in a time of suffering to give hope. Can you tell the story of Jeremiah's response in that text and why it's important?

GG: It's impossible really to summarize this briefly. Jeremiah was in a very bad situation. Two political powers were fighting and then the King of Judah exiled him to prison. In that crucial moment, one person arrived from his family to offer him the purchase of his uncle's land. According to the laws of the time, Jeremiah had the first option to buy or not buy his relative's land. It was a decision that not only symbolized the people's crisis but addressed it through the powers of law of the country. So Jeremiah thought this was a message from God. Even in this solitary situation, one without hope, he must do this concrete action to buy the land. "This will signify to the people that it's possible to do something in spite of the bad situation." Both in the text and today, we have Jeremiah buying this land and then more. In our very difficult situation today, we must buy land and even do something very modest or insignificant. The point is to inspire hope.

In terms of the project in northern Rwanda, financial investors would not have said, "This is the piece of land where you should build something." On the other hand, we see this idea of Jeremiah that if you build something on the land, it will give hope. How do the people in that area react to this?

PF: Rwanda right now is a place where smart investors, to push your metaphor, probably would invest. It has been seventeen years since the genocide. Haiti is a place that reminds me more of the scene described in Jeremiah. With the Haitian Ministry of Health and other local partners, we are going into central Haiti and building a big teaching hospital.

The Jeremiah story speaks to me because this hospital will be the same manifestation of hope. We believe in Haiti's ability to recover, but not only that. We believe that although the nursing school, the medical school, and the health professional training sites were damaged or destroyed in the 2010 earthquake, we are going to rebuild them, and we are going to invest for the next several decades because we know that we are going to put our stakes down for the long-term. Every time we make a long term investment, start a new training program, or plant a tree, it is another manifestation of this hope. One day your sapling will shade people—probably not me—but it will be here, it will grow, and it will be a towering tree some day.

GG: It is not enough to say that you must have hope, but also to demonstrate it with acts and gestures.

Moving from one biblical figure to another, I would like to ask about Job. Gustavo, you have mentioned how important your book on Job is to you personally, and we spoke about the distinctions among the suffering, the innocent, and the guilty, and about hope. For you, Job emerges as a very important figure in confronting the suffering of poverty. Can you say a little bit about why Job is so important to the suffering of the poor?

GG: First of all, my concern with and my interest in reading and reflecting again and again on the Book of Job comes from my experience as a parish priest where the suffering of the poor is very present. I mentioned before briefly the question of the little girls and little boys in my parish. They are born into terrible circumstances, and they are very vulnerable. So I was working on the book *On Job* with my community in the parish. The book was for explaining and discussing these circumstances. I was not looking for solutions, but rather how to deal with this question.

In the Book of Job, we have the presence of theologians, Job's comforters, but the Book of Job is not trying to deal with the question of evil in history. In some manner, it directs us more or less to live with this problem. Its author, this great theologian whose name we don't know, tried to say, "God loves us mysteriously, yet unceasingly." As Job understands the book, in discussing the question, this conflict is always present—the constant presence of God, and the future love of God in the presence of the problem of suffering. Trying to eliminate the suffering is only one answer. It is too much to say trying to fight against the suffering. Being close to the persons suffering, or accompanying, is the only other possibility. It is not a typical answer. Suffering has no meaning in this sense. It is important because even today with the witness of Jesus, for some people, suffering is the means to save us. It is not so. It is love, not suffering. Suffering was the price to pay for announcing the Kingdom of God. Jesus accepted to pay this price, but for what? For love. We have no other reason than this.

Suffering is a mystery. We must accept this and not lose fortitude in working toward peace. I struggled with this, for a long time, even today, but I read all the books of Albert Camus about the matter of how a nonbeliever can understand evil. I am also trying to understand a little about this question of the meaning of suffering without belief in God. I find it so deep and so human to confront suffering and to experience its consequences for a sense of my life. The suffering of the innocent is a subject in all the books of Camus, but is very well known in the novel *The Plague*. I think it is important to confront who is suffering and confront our fates in God. We say love is God; well, it is joy in confronting suffering as well.

PF: Well, one of my favorite books is your study of the Book of Job, which I read in Haiti. It came out in 1987. I was finishing my thesis, which soon would become my first book, and used it heavily in my work. I am glad to hear you say it was a mystery because I find the Book of Job almost impenetrable, and I use your book to help me interpret this "mysterious" suffering. I'd like to hear what you think, because I think most suffering is not a mystery. It's structural violence, which, as you know, puts some people at risk of outrageous fates while protecting others

GG: Gabriel Marcel, the French philosopher, distinguished between the categories of mystery and problem. For him, a mystery is not just something that he does not understand. It is a matter one has insight into, but there is a reason we cannot know it fully. We know something about suffering. But it is not a problem to be solved. I think of mystery not as something of which I understand nothing, but something which I have insight into, as we call God a mystery.

PF: Mystery in the theological sense. Going back to Camus and *The Plague*—one of the things that is so striking in my work is that almost no epidemic is a mystery. The microbes always make this preferential option for the poor with every epidemic from cholera in Peru to AIDS in Africa to tuberculosis in a Siberian prison. It's very helpful to me to understand that. You know, I struggled with your book on Job.

GG: Job is struggling with God. Job was struggling. Jeremiah was struggling with God also in Chapter 32. I think the true believers are struggling with God.

PF: Well, that's good news for me. I struggle a lot.

GG: Struggling is not refusing; it's just struggling.

You bring out very clearly, Gustavo, that Job finally places his faith in the hands of God. For you, that is spiritual childhood, and what it means to be poor in spirit, yet that obviously does not mean to abandon responsibility in history. In your work, Paul, is that tension ever resolved? What does it look like to place our fates in the hands of God but still maintain a responsibility to history?

PF: I assume the equivalent of being a parish priest is being a doctor because you hear the same kinds of Jeremiah-like or Job-like complaints about the very practical pain and suffering—no housing, no food, no land, being tormented and vilified by the powerful. The structure and agency part of it helps me, in any case, by saying that we want to attack poverty, we want to go to the roots of this suffering. We do have, again, the practical ministry of showing up, which for a parish priest, is one thing; for a doctor or nurse, another. That means we, as doctors and nurses, say, "Well, here are the things we can do to help you, Job, with your skin affliction." I think Job needed a good dermatologist.

That isn't sacrilegious, is it? There are some practical things that could be done, and that's what Partners In Health tries to do. We shuttle between the practical services that people ask us for, but also try to get at these deep-rooted causes. In that praxis is also reflection on suffering, tackling the hard questions of theodicy like Job did in his conversations. There's a humility that comes out of realizing that, in spite of a lifetime of effort, you might not alter the life chances of as many people as you want, but there are things you could do for the person who's talking about his or her suffering right in front of you. Does that make sense?

I feel that for you, Job is a model of humility.

GG: He was a fighter, but humble and accepting as a fighter, which is another reason I love the Book of Job most in the Bible. The second one is the gospel of John. John is very ironical. Reading and rereading the Book of Job is another thing.

Moving from Beneath

Both of you share the methodology of starting from below. Because of this, both of you have also encountered resistance from your respective establishments. I'd like to ask Paul: In your experience, why did you choose to start from below? I'm hoping you'll speak about what's really going on when people talk about noncompliance, and how if you take seriously the experience of the poor, it yields a whole different set of conclusions.

PF: It is perhaps easier to start with a subversive approach in medicine than in theology. The burden of disease is clearly among the poor, so when you follow the pathology in medicine and in public health, you are doing your job. I don't want to exaggerate the resistance. The resistance I have met has largely been in the field when you're disrupting local social orders—in Haiti, and even in Lima. I feel very rewarded academically, and I'm very grateful to my university for recognizing that this work is important to medicine. But back to the epiphanies that changed my life in terms of methodology.

I have mentioned already that I was reading Gustavo's work and that of others as I was starting in Haiti. There are also some very inspiring figures in social medicine. Maybe you've read about Rudolph Virchow, the great nineteenth-century doctor. He was not only a pathologist but a father of medical anthropology who was engaged on behalf of the poor in places like Upper Silesia. I regard, for example, the work we are doing now with Cuban and Haitian faculty in Haiti to promote social medicine as very much in that tradition. These are important insights whether you are a pathologist or an oncologist or an infectious disease doctor or a psychiatrist or pediatrician.

One thing that has troubled me a lot and still does all over the world, is that the local providers—doctors, priests, the nonpoor—often said, "Well, you know, for people to value this service, they have to pay for it." I cannot tell you how many times I've heard this in Africa and Asia and Boston and everywhere, but I *never* heard it from the patients. No one ever said to me, "You know, for me to value this medical care, I really need to pay you something." Now, grateful patients would give me gifts like chickens and bottles full of God-knows-what, but never said this. I heard this alleged mostly by my peers. By peers, I mean people like Gustavo, me, and people who were not poor but who were working right there with me in the clinic.

The tuberculosis clinic in Cange was where I learned how to think critically about compliance. When we put in place a formulary for the diagnosis and treatment of tuberculosis, we insisted, in keeping with international recommendations, that these, at least, we were not going to sell. The care of tuberculosis was a "public good for public health" or, to use rights language, a basic human right. Anybody with tuberculosis is going to get free care. In 1988, the same year, by the way, that two of those three young people died—the young woman with cerebral malaria and the young man with typhoid fever—we lost three other patients to tuberculosis. I had already been working in Haiti for five years and was in the middle of of my medical and anthropology training at Harvard. We had this meeting of the doctors and nurses and the community health workers. The meeting was to say, "Okay, what happened? Why, in 1988, or maybe '87, do we have three people die of a completely treatable disease right here in our clinic, with its so-called free TB care?

What happened next was a debate: the professionals versus the community health workers, who we called *accompagnateurs*. The *accompagnateurs* shared the social conditions of the patients. All of them were poor people. The professionals might have said, "Oh no, Paul, we don't share your social conditions," but they really did. They went to medical or nursing school, they read and wrote, they spoke more than one language, usually French and Haitian and maybe a little English. That was the split, a class divide. So when the professionals said, "The problem is the patients are noncompliant; they're superstitious; they don't believe in modern medicine," the *accompagnateurs* added a nuance: "No, no that is not it at all. They may be superstitious, but that is not why they died of tuberculosis. They died of tuberculosis because of barriers to getting here for diagnosis and remaining in treatment for two years." I said, "Well, how could that be true? They're from the same villages as you. There are no fees." It turned out that for each of these patients, as for all of the patients who lived in poverty, there were other barriers that the professionals couldn't see. For example, these patients didn't have enough food. We were saying that our definition of medicine is: Here's the diagnosis, here's the treatment. Take it. But we needed to go further, you know, we needed to listen more.

When we actually went out and did what we said we were doing, which was listening to the poor, we discovered that we weren't listening enough. So when we went and listened more, we heard them say, "I can't get to the clinic, the hours are inconvenient. I don't have someone to take care of my children while I am gone to clinic. I don't have enough to eat. I don't have a donkey to get me there." (How biblical is that, Gustavo, no donkeys? That will be the name of my next book, *Where There Is No Donkey*.) When we started addressing these structural problems, as opposed to things that were related only to individual patients or to the culture, mortality rates dropped. No more patients died of TB, not from those villages. Imagine, even after several years of reading and thinking, there's still more you can learn about how to structure a program by actually listening to people.

Conclusion

I'll close with this question for Gustavo. Can you describe how you came to see the experience of the poor as a theological locus? I know you aren't the first to do so, but you certainly have become identified with starting from the experience of the poor. Why did you adopt that method when so many others of your generation did not?

GG: Poverty, ultimately, means an early and unjust death. Poverty is not only a social issue. It is a human issue, and consequently a challenge to faith and thus a challenge to theology. I said earlier that we have several approaches to poverty, but the most important approach comes from direct contact with the poor. In my life, reflection about that started very early, with my own family, in my country, and after that as a priest in the poor neighborhoods of Lima. All these were very relevant. Poverty is a theological challenge because it is a human, or rather an inhuman situation. Bartolomé de las Casas in the sixteenth century said about the Indians that they were dying before their time.[1] This is happening with the poor today. Las Casas attempted to organize the Indians into autonomous villages on the pattern of Dominican communities, as a way of protecting them from colonial exploitation, but not even he could save them. (These communities were taken over by other monastic orders.) Even today it is not so easy to understand the theological challenge coming from poverty. Taking up from Las Casas, who saw that early and unjust death was a theological challenge, I have attempted to show that poverty is a subject inherent to theology, no mere social problem, and by keeping the topic alive in the church I try to make it clearer and clearer.

PF: I'm thinking back to some of your reminders that we have to create hope. The great defeater of hope is death, death that statistically correlates with poverty. That is an epidemiological fact, it is a demographic fact, it is, as you say, a spiritual fact, and a human fact. But starting from that. . . .

GG: A cultural fact.

PF: It is a cultural fact. And starting from the point that poverty is death, I think one of the ways that we can create hope is by saying that poverty becomes embodied as high risk of disease and poor outcomes once sick. Where we can intervene through medicine and public health, we have a way of saying, "We might not be undoing poverty by making sure we have high-quality medical care, but once we get this specific manifestation of poverty out of your body, that will leave you free to fight on against poverty." If you're dead, you're not fighting.

GG: We distinguish between physical, economic, and also cultural poverty. The only trouble is that people like to say culture is life. When we despise a culture, we are killing the people belonging to this culture. It is physical death, but cultural also. Little by little we are coming to understand cultural death, and to see it as very important. Culture death is a theological issue for many reasons, but the central reason is because it is, theologically speaking, against God's will in favor of life. The creation is one instance of the will to life, of the creation of life; and poverty is really a failure to honor the creation. This sentence is not mine, I'm quoting it from a former general of the Jesuit Order. Poverty is a failure to follow the will of God as a will for life; poverty is against this will to realize the creation, a very theological issue, an issue occupying at least the same level as modernity's challenge to theology. Many people seem to think that modernity is the great challenge to theology. Well, modernity is not only philosophical wisdom, human wisdom set up as a rival to the theological. Consider the case of poverty. Poverty today is our challenge, as an economic question, as a medical question, but it becomes a question and challenge for theology in this practical sense. This is exactly how I mean that it is a theological challenge. We need to rethink the Christian message. That message is couched in the terms of theology, but more than theology, what we need is to rethink the Christian message from the perspective of the challenge coming from modernity. Theology is very historical. It is dependent on the moment to find the right language to speak of God; this is theology.

If you had a message to communicate to undergraduates today about where you come from, what is important to you, and what you are doing, what would you say?

PF: The main thing I can tell undergraduates as a teacher of graduate students and doctors is that the path that I am on now and the things that I am doing all started for me when I was a college student, when I took a class in medical anthropology. Of course, that classroom experience was linked to practical responses to the suffering of people living in poverty, first in my own neighborhood, which, at that time, happened to be North Carolina, and then in the broader world. I started as a student, and what I was studying could have been anthropology, it could have been theology, it could have been almost any field that informs service. It could have been any kind of service such as teaching kids in an inner-city school. The first point is that I started doing this in college, and the second point is there are many ways to do it. The third, and the reason why I am here today, is that your inspiration can come from unlikely sources. Certainly I took a lot of guidance from Father Gustavo and others who write in that tradition, which was not typical of anthropologists or physicians at that moment.

You are teaching your final class, and in your last minutes of class, you want to get your message across to your students. What is the most important thing you want to communicate?

GG: Well, the grammar book of any language will tell you that the first person is "I," "I am." I think the first person is "you are," and after we have recognized that you are, we can say, "I am." The philosopher Emmanuel Levinas calls this the priority of the ethical over the epistemological. First you establish a relation with the other, and then you have a basis for choosing to pursue knowledge, knowledge of this rather than that, and so on. How we should be toward others, not what we can know, is the central question of philosophy. From this follow many applications: how to be open, to know reality, to be sensitive to the suffering of other persons, and so on. I think it is very, very important to take this point of view.

I'd like to ask Paul if he can say how Gustavo has helped him become a better doctor in his vocation, not as theologian, but as doctor.

PF: I would say, just as Gustavo has helped us understand how poverty is both a scandal and the chief issue for theological reflection, I think inequality and poverty are the chief human rights questions of our times. Medicine has many powerful tools, but we're not going to be able to use them justly without a plan to attack poverty—we need more ways of making a preferential option for the poor in health care to be better doctors. I'm very grateful to you, Gustavo.

GG: And I to you, for your creativity in dealing with this issue in your area.

Notes

¹ Bartolomé de las Casas (1484–1566) was an early participant in the Spanish conquest of the Americas who was scandalized by the murder and slavery practiced by the conquerors. An attempt at creating a peaceful colony was cut short, and he entered the Dominican order. His *Short Account of the Destruction of the Indies* (1542, published 1552) attempted to bring to the attention of the Spanish court the inhumanity of the colonial administration.

Afterword

Steve Reifenberg

Setting the Stage

In the large, first floor atrium of the University of Notre Dame's Main Building, four stories below the famed golden dome, students gathered around Paul Farmer and Ophelia Dahl, co-founders of Partners In Health (PIH), eagerly hoping to engage the two figures they find so inspiring.

Earlier that day, April 27, 2011, PIH had been awarded the University of Notre Dame's Award for International Human Development and Solidarity.[1] At the ceremony, Dahl and Farmer had commented that the award, rather than representing individual achievement, recognized the work of some 13,000 PIH employees and an ever-expanding network of partners and supporters worldwide. Dahl and Farmer then addressed a packed Washington Hall auditorium, one of the largest on campus, about their global health work that focuses on caring for patients, working to alleviate the root causes of disease, and sharing lessons learned.

At a reception that followed in the Main Building, Farmer asked eight or so students what they were studying. Most said they were science students, interested in going to medical school; some had additional minors in poverty studies or anthropology or peace studies.

"You are so lucky to be here at Notre Dame," Farmer told the group, and all nodded energetically. "It must be incredible to have the chance to study with Gustavo Gutiérrez," he added. "It's amazing just to have him here in your presence."

The animated, engaged conversation slowed down. No one said anything. A few students shuffled their feet. Farmer scanned their faces.

"You do know . . . ," he paused, then pronouncing each word slowly asked, "You do know about Father Gutiérrez?" Not a single student among his enthusiastic followers said anything.

"Tell me it's not so. . . . Anyone? Liberation theology? Padre Gustavo? What do they teach you here at Notre Dame?"

As if starting from scratch, he began describing this mentor who had such an impact on his life and his work. "Okay. Father Gustavo teaches here at Notre Dame half the year, and lives the other half in Peru. His ideas form the foundation for much of our work at Partners In Health," he said, scanning the faces for some kind of connection.

"Let me try again. It is kind of like having Yoda from Star Wars, right here on campus for half the year. You smile, yes," he said to them, "but it's true. Hear me out. . . . Padre Gustavo and Yoda have a lot in common—they are both short and wrinkled and wise."

Rather than rebuke, he encouraged the students with a plea. If they were interested in issues of poverty and global health— just the kind of things he knew they cared about—then they needed to familiarize themselves with Father Gustavo's work.

"You should get to know the amazing Father Gustavo himself," Farmer said. "He will rock your world."

Perhaps it is not surprising that a group of students committed to science might know little about Father Gutiérrez and liberation theology, as science and theology aren't always fluid partners in dialogue. (In Notre Dame's defense, during the same visit, Farmer got to know other science students, who had studied personally with the inspiring theologian from Peru, and he had, in fact, rocked their world.)

Farmer's encouragement to that group of students for greater awareness of Father Gustavo's work became the seed of the dialogue on "Reimagining Accompaniment: Liberation Theology and Global Health" that was hosted at Notre Dame some seven months later, in October 2011. At the event Farmer continued his spirited exhortation to come into the power of Father Gustavo's vision. And this book itself has something of that same enthusiastic encouragement, not only to become familiar with these ideas, but to realize how transforming they can be, and, possibly, to see them as the seeds of a new social movement.

We Drink from Our Own Wells

In these dialogues, there is obvious joy for both Gutiérrez and Farmer, two friends with deep respect for one another, drawing off the different experiences and insights of the other. As I read the manuscript, especially the dialogues, I was inspired, indignant (at the state of the world), and at times laughed out loud. If you've gotten this far reading the book, you're fully aware that while there are many similarities between the two protagonists, there are also some notable differences.

Gutiérrez was ordained a priest in 1959, the year that Farmer was born, and Gutiérrez whole-heartedly understands and interprets the world from a religious and spiritual perspective. "A conversion is the starting point of every spiritual journey," he begins his chapter on "Conversion: A Requirement for Solidarity." "It involves a break with the life lived up to that point; it is a prerequisite for entering the kingdom: 'The time is fulfilled and the kingdom of God is at hand; repent, and believe in the gospel' (Mk 1:15),"[2] Gutiérrez writes.

Farmer's stance toward religion is decidedly more mixed. He grew up bored by organized religion, finding his Catholic upbringing of little relevance in helping understand the world around him. In college, it was seeing the concrete works of Catholic nuns working with the poor that led him to reevaluate his own religious tradition and see insights he had not seen there before. Gutiérrez later was especially helpful in giving

an intellectual foundation, drawing Farmer into an appreciation for liberation theology with its emphasis on poverty and
injustice, and its challenge to do something concrete about
them.

Farmer and Gutiérrez often present similar concepts, but
with different vocabulary. "The stubbornness we often find in
the great saints," Gutiérrez writes, "is nothing but the expression of a profound fidelity that does not bow to difficulties and
obstacles."[3] On the same point Farmer suggests, "Persistence is
the secret sauce."

But as this volume suggests, there is much that connects this
still youngish Harvard-educated doctor in his early fifties and
a Peruvian priest in his mid eighties. Before he realized he was
going to be a priest, Gutiérrez began studying in the faculty
of medicine of the National University of San Marcus in Peru
in order to become a psychiatrist. Both studied in France and
were deeply influenced by European intellectual traditions. At
the same time, both lives connected in direct and personal ways
with the poor who influence almost everything they do, teach,
and write. Both share a deep and abiding admiration for Archbishop Oscar Romero from El Salvador and Romero's belief that
"an authentic Christian conversion must lead to an unmasking
of the social mechanisms that turn the worker and peasant into
marginalized persons."[4]

Gutiérrez often poses the challenge, gently and not so gently, of advancing *hermeneutics*—the art and science of interpretation—to the world around us. "Extending a hermeneutic of
generosity to those who rely more on a hermeneutic of suspicion . . . has been an enduring intellectual and personal project
for me," Farmer writes. I similarly imagine it is a project for all
of us. Gutiérrez furthermore taught him to look for the hermeneutic of hope that might follow the hermeneutic of generosity.
"Through every defeat and every small victory," Farmer states,
"liberation theology and Gustavo's writing have remained a real
touchstone for me."[5]

Farmer writes that he has distilled from Gutiérrez three simple points on the preferential option for the poor. First, material poverty is never good but is rather an evil to be opposed. Second, poverty is due to structural injustices that privilege some while marginalizing others. Third, poverty is a complex reality and is not limited to its economic dimension. To be poor is to be insignificant. Poverty means an early and unjust death.

This analysis of poverty leads both Gutiérrez and Farmer to highlight the elements of a response: a commitment to standing with the poor against the causes of poverty; listening, humility, and hope; that theology and medicine both require "practical ministry"; and ultimately, the conviction that we all live in *one* world.

Gutiérrez suggests there is often a disconnect between a person's spirituality and social justice, between the inner world of a person and the outer world of poverty, and between mysticism and prophecy. We cannot truly listen to the words of scripture, he says, and not be concerned for the poor and oppressed. "This is a criterion for knowing whether God is close to us or far away," Gutiérrez observes, quoting Archbishop Romero; "all those who worry about the hungry, the naked, the poor, the disappeared, the tortured, the imprisoned—about any suffering human being—are close to God."[6]

Gutiérrez encourages us not only to root spirituality in our own experience, but also in the cries of the poor. "Drinking from our own wells," suggests grounding spirituality in one's own experience, and especially in the experience of the poor and their struggle for life. Drinking from our own wells does not imply that we *only* draw nourishment from our own tradition and local situation. While emphasizing something that is personal, particular, and local, there is also a universal dimension.

Both Gutiérrez and Farmer share the view that important ideas can and must cross traditions and geographies. Woven through this volume is Farmer's encouragement that we draw from these deep insights of liberation theology, that invite us all in, whether followers of a Christian tradition or not, to identify with the plight of the poor, address the root causes of poverty, and work to mitigate their suffering.

Accompaniment in Action

Both Gutiérrez and Farmer invite us into their work—in theology and global health—and offer a model of how to make solidarity operational: *accompaniment.*

"This attitude of God must serve as a model for the people of God," Gutiérrez writes. "As Micah puts it, 'He has showed you, O man, what is good; and what does the Lord require of you but to do justice, and to love kindness, and to walk humbly with your God?' (6:8)."[7] There is an urgency to the message—walk humbly together, with God and with one another, in search of justice and mercy.

"'Accompaniment' is an elastic term," Farmer writes in *Foreign Affairs.* "It has a basic, everyday meaning. To accompany someone is to go somewhere with him or her, to break bread together, to be present on a journey with a beginning and an end. There's an element of mystery, of openness, of trust, in accompaniment. The companion, the *accompagnateur*, says: 'I'll go with you and support you on your journey wherever it leads; I'll share your fate for a while. And by "a while," I don't mean a little while.' Accompaniment is about sticking with a task until it's deemed completed, not by the *accompagnateur* but by the person being accompanied."[8]

Yet accompaniment is not simply walking together. It requires recognizing real-world complexities, acknowledging the asymmetries of power and privilege, and being willing to address these *while walking together.* There is something fundamentally but beautifully radical in this idea. In a society so focused on individual attributes and achievement, this simple concept of walking beside another, humbly and ever toward justice, could change the world. In the words of Mother Teresa, "The problem with the world is that we draw the circle of our family too small." This dialogue is about drawing ever larger circles, encompassing us in a radically wider conception of family, from Peru to Haiti to Rwanda and back to the United States, on college campuses and inner cities, in local parishes and in medical schools.

This same accompaniment concept can also be applied to the relationships between nations. What is needed, Farmer argues, is a new social movement that changes the way countries and institutions have traditionally thought about development aid—moving, in Farmer's words, "from Aid to Accompaniment."

Envisioning international development aid as "accompaniment"—that we're in this together, and not just for a little while, but for the long run—would call us to identify and support institutions that truly represent the poor; partner with public institutions rather than "go it alone"; make job creation a benchmark of success; invest directly in the poor themselves; and establish learning loops that put in practice what we learn through this accompaniment process. "True accompaniment does not privilege technical expertise above solidarity, compassion, and a willingness to tackle what may seem insuperable challenges," writes Farmer. "It requires cooperation, openness, and humility; this concept may, I hope, infuse new vitality into development work."

Gutiérrez describes Jesus in the Acts of the Apostles passing through this world "doing good." "Jesus not only healed the sick, Jesus allowed the sick to take part of their own healing. Very often Jesus told them: 'your faith had saved you.' Once healed, they became, also, agents of healing, and an invitation to be agents of their own destiny."

In Peru, accompaniment in practice is a community health worker who lives in a shantytown outside of Lima, daily climbing up and down the dusty hills of a settlement. During her home visits, she not only watches the person she is accompanying take the necessary tuberculosis medication and discusses basic health care; she also probably discusses daily life, ranging from counseling what to do with a misbehaving teenager (be patient) and what to do about an errant husband (don't be *too* patient). She visits every single day, because if you're a TB patient, it's critical that you don't miss a treatment. Many community health workers are former TB patients themselves, and for some, it is their first-ever paid job. Today nearly two-thirds of 13,000 people working for PIH around the globe are community health workers—*accompagnateurs*. Poor people who now have jobs, which in and of itself is transformative, and they in turn, through their work, transform the lives of others.

Accompaniment provides not only a reimagination for those who work on and think about global health but also an emerging framework that can be applied, to use Gutiérrez's term, in *mil maneras*—a thousand ways—from housing to education, economics to environmental policy, food security to peace promotion.

Accompaniment flips the impulse of "how do we help them?" into an assertion—"we're in this together." We are connected, tied, and bound together. We need to walk together and learn together, and maybe, together, we can envision and create better, more equitable tomorrows, both for the big issues "over there" and also in our daily lives, loving our neighbors—that is, everyone—as we love ourselves.

Although one aspiration of this book is to make more visible the linkages between liberation theology and global health, another is to expand the dialogue outward, encouraging us to think that this is not *just* a dialogue on liberation theology and global health. Here within are the seeds of a new social movement centered on accompaniment. In this way, global health can be seen as one inspiring path—one of the thousand ways—to make one's preferential option for the poor a journey of walking together.

Notes

[1] Awarded by the Ford Family Program for Human Development Studies and Solidarity of Notre Dame's Kellogg Institute for International Studies.

[2] Gustavo Gutiérrez, *We Drink from Our Own Wells: The Spiritual Journey of a People* (1984; Maryknoll, NY: Orbis Books, 2003), 95.

[3] Ibid., 105.

[4] Ibid., 98.

[5] Farmer–Gutiérrez interview at Notre Dame, October 24, 2011.

[6] Archbishop Oscar Romero, homily, February 5, 1978, quoted in Gustavo Gutiérrez, "The Option for the Poor Arises from Faith in Christ."

[7] Gutiérrez, *We Drink from Our Own Wells*, 100.

[8] Paul Farmer, "Partners In Help: Assisting the Poor Over the Long-Term," *Foreign Affairs*, July 29, 2011, 4.

Index